WTF –
Wake Up, Transform, Flourish

Attain the Wealth You De$erve and Live LARGE

Patrick Murray

WTF – WAKE UP, TRANSFORM, FLOURISH

Copyright © 2016 by Patrick Murray

All rights reserved. This book or any portion thereof may not be reproduced or used in any manner whatsoever without the express written permission of the publisher except for the use of brief quotations in a book review.

Table of Contents

Introduction 5

Wake Up 17

    Chapter 1: Overcome Your Story 18

    Chapter 2: Burn and Learn 31

    Chapter 3: Don't Worry; Be Happy 44

    Chapter 4: Social Impact 54

Transform 67

    Chapter 5: Empower 68

    Chapter 6: Shift 79

    Chapter 7: Thrive with Gratitude 86

    Chapter 8: Your Untapped Power Within 97

Flourish 108

Chapter 9: The Compass 109

Chapter 10: Reset 126

Chapter 11: Fly 135

WTF: A Brief Re-Cap 143

Closing 149

Appendix 152

Introduction

"It's not the mountain that we conquer, but ourselves."

- Sir Edmund Hillary

I don't know you, but I am going to ask you this very pointed question:

Are you happy?

I want you to dig deep. Are you truly happy with your life or are you living somebody else's life? Are you living your life in alignment with your beliefs?

Can you answer who are you? What about why were you put on this earth?

These are questions that need answering if you truly want to attain the wealth you deserve and live large. There is a caveat to all of these questions and it is that only *you* can truly answer them. These aren't queries to be quickly passed over. They require careful introspection on your part. And it's okay if you don't have the answers to these questions just yet.

Let's delve a little deeper.

Do you have a stomach ache on Sunday night because you have to return to work on Monday morning? Do you feel as though you are chronically stuck in a situation, whether work or personal, and it makes you unhappy? Do you feel that you have hit rock bottom and that you don't feel that you have any purpose for betterment and enjoyment of your life? Are you often worried and fearful? If you answer any of these questions in the affirmative, then you need to examine more closely the questions above.

Don't worry about this, though; you are not alone. I would dare to say that the majority of people that you interact with on a daily basis feel they are in the very same situation. This means that the vast majority of the population is, to some extent, unhappy in some way. You can see it in the way people interact with one another. It's apparent in their speech and in their demeanour as a whole. It's a very troubling realization. If you are asking the questions, then you are seeking the answers. You know there must be more to life. Know that I am writing this book for you because I was once starting to seek these answers myself.

If you can answer the above questions and be completely satisfied with your answers, then you will not only realize true happiness as it was meant to be experienced, but radiate as a positive human being to those around you. You will want to go to work. You will want to interact with those in your life because you will focus on flourishing with people that are like-minded. You will have very satisfying and connected relationships. You will be healthier and wealthier. You will have a clear direction for your life. You will create the life you want simply because you seek it and take action towards it. You will succeed and you will attain the wealth you deserve.

What I Once Looked Like

There is teaching and there is doing. Many teach, but never do. Of those that do, few teach. I'm happy to tell you that I have taken this journey and now I want to share it with you. I want you to understand where I have been and, as this book goes on, you will see where I am now. To do this I will have to be very open and honest with you. I have a rule that I apply to others. I cannot judge another because I have not taken the same journey. This does not mean that I have nothing to offer you. On the contrary, learning from another's journey is an excellent way of understanding our own journey. This applies to one's past and to one's future.

My Roots

I come from a strict Protestant upbringing from a small city in Saskatchewan, Canada. I am the seventh of seven children. I have four sisters and two brothers. The oldest is nineteen and a half years older than I, and the youngest is nine and a half years older than myself. In a way, I was an only child by the age of nine. Even now, many of my siblings seem more like good family friends than siblings to me.

Luckily, I had wonderful parents. My father was a respected school principal and had me when he was forty and my mother was thirty-eight. My mother was a part-time stay-at-home mom and a nursery school teacher. I was always very aware that my parents were much older than those of my friends. Having children later in life is pretty common now, but stress had also taken a toll on my parents for various reasons, which made them seem even older. I had tremendous love and respect for my parents. I know that they loved me very much even though we weren't financially well off. I was always aware of how tight money was and I felt that my parents made sure I knew it. Both of them had many health issues as I grew up and became an adult. To some extent, their health issues affected my upbringing. Mom and Dad wanted the best for me, always saying that I could do whatever I put my mind to and could become anything I wanted to become. On the other hand, there was the very over-protective side of my parents and it came out more in my teenage years and later in adulthood. While they wanted what was best for me, I think they wanted what they *felt* was best for me.

Maybe you have heard this sentiment: "Oh you can't do that! That's too risky!" "Be careful. That's not a very good idea." "You go to school, get a good job and save for your retirement." In a way, I was afraid to make a move without first consulting my parents. In large part, I believe that it's because I wanted to please them and was simply fearful of disappointing them, of letting them down. Perhaps it was because of the many health issues that my parents endured, but I often felt guilty if I didn't live up to their expectations. Part of me now knows that this was unintentional projection on their part.

I also learned a lot about sacrifice from an early age. With my parents having the health issues that they had, I wasn't necessarily the happy-go-lucky kid some of my friends were. Not that I wasn't ever happy, but I was fairly introverted. I did a fair bit of caring for Mom and Dad, or picking up the slack at home with some prodding from my parents. I didn't party. I didn't drink. I obeyed my parents. I kept it very low key.

Keep in mind that I'm not complaining here. This is simply how I grew up.

I also went through three years of childhood depression from the age of thirteen to fifteen. It was a difficult period for me, which involved a falling out with a close family member. I accepted responsibility for my part in this, but it turns out that there was so much more going. It was troubling me to figure out what was truly happening. It was a situation where I thought, and felt I was led to believe, that I was completely responsible. Once I became an adult I realized that it was true family politics at play and yet it wasn't spoken about. I felt like I was more or less a pawn and I think those involved still have no idea of the effect this occurrence had on me as a child and how it has affected me in adulthood. I felt that nobody let me out of, what I considered, my own personal hell. I felt I was in the dark. I felt I was hung out to dry by the people that I loved and cared about. I felt used and worthless. In conjunction with the stress with my parents' health, my Mom just had brain surgery to remove a tumour and her chances of surviving the surgery were slim. It simply became too much for me. I didn't know why I existed and I didn't want to exist. I was in a dark place, isolated from my peers and my family. I felt like an outcast.

I ask that you please don't think that I am comparing my childhood to others who had many more challenges than I, because that is not my goal here. I love my parents with all of my heart and soul and I know that they loved me. Mom and Dad did the best they could and these experiences made me who I am today. For that, I am thankful. My writings here are merely intended to give my history showing that all of us have a story.

When I was leaving secondary school I had a pretty good idea what I wanted to do with my life. I wanted to be an athletic trainer with a professional sports team. I chose to go to university two hours away from home at the University of Saskatchewan. When I arrived at school I realized that my dream was going to be very difficult to achieve as so many others also had this very same dream. What I thought would be my unique calling was not all that unique. It was actually quite competitive. It was also at this time that my parents left the church that we always attended and for which we were very involved, to attend another church. To me it was almost like changing religions. Even though they were still Protestants, this change made me confused. I felt like I had lost a lot of my hard earned friends.

It was around this time that I realized that the family politics from my past really had little to do with me and so it was a very angry time for me in my life. I wondered how anybody could let a child slip through the cracks and go through what I went through. It was beyond me. I felt like others in my family knew more, but would not share with me. Did everybody think I was so naïve that I wouldn't figure out the truth about the family politics and that I didn't need to suffer as I had? I found that my family just did not speak of such things. I became rebellious. I quickly learned about partying and alcohol and fighting. In the end, the university asked me to take a year off and the family with whom I was living with (old friends of my parents and a policeman) kicked me out of their house for my partying ways. I was lost. I felt like a failure and a huge disappointment to my parents. I lacked confidence in myself. I had no idea what I would do, but I knew that I did not want to return to live with my parents. I couldn't go backwards. To go forwards, I had to get a job and support myself.

I disliked many of the jobs that I felt were menial and were merely a way for me to scrape by at the time. That's when I decided I wanted to do something that would help me advance myself, be happy, and become financially secure. I didn't know what position offered the answer, but my big brother was a funeral director for his entire working life and I thought I could do the job, too. Maybe this occupation would be my calling? I did it, but I was young and got all of the grunt work of cleaning cars and the chapel. I was passed over a few too many times for promotions given my youth and moved onto a new position as a chauffeur with a limousine service. I really liked my employer, but I drank way too much (never behind the wheel!) and partied more than I should have. I also ended up getting married around this time and, while I didn't know it, was much too early an age for me to get married. I got another job as a flight attendant and liked the job, but endured a few lay-offs in a short amount of time. For those reasons, I didn't feel that this would be a stable earning environment. It was at this time when my then wife and I moved to Vancouver for my airline job. But, as much as I loved it, she hated it. We moved back to the Prairies where I took a management job at Blockbuster Video while I went to school to better my education and applied to become a dental hygienist. Just as I was starting my dental hygiene schooling, my marriage ended. This made me the first person in my family to be divorced. Hitting me quite hard, I was told that marriage is forever and if all of my siblings and my parents could do it, why couldn't I do it? Did I mention my strict Protestant upbringing?

I didn't know how I would be able to look my family in the face again. Already lacking in self-confidence and questioning my worth as a person because of my past, I once again felt like a huge failure.

Now, as much as there was pain during this time, I did have the good fortune of meeting my now wife while in Dental Hygiene school. Together, we moved to Calgary, Alberta, dated and, 5 years later, we married. From the very beginning, she has always been a great supporter of me. A few years after we married, we decided we wanted to start a family. That same month, my wife had a serious health scare and our plans were on hold, possibly forever. I was terrified of losing her as she went through intense medical treatment for over a year. It was during this same year that my father, who had always had health issues, had a massive heart attack and died at the age of 73. I was so thankful to have my wife, yet at the same time I was devastated that a man that had so much influence over my life was gone. It was a very tough year. We ate into our savings and our credit line to help us through this challenging time. While my wife had disability insurance, I wasn't working much because I wanted to be with her and, simply enough, she needed me. It was a challenging time emotionally and financially for both of us, but I never regret being with her as much as I was. Perspective was a big lesson that year. Now, by the way, she's fine!

This became an eye opening epiphany. We realized how short life can be and that we needed to make the most of our lives. While we liked practicing dental hygiene, we didn't like the business influence of dentistry, which seemed to foreshadow the health care we were qualified to provide. Both of us had been unhappy at work for some time. In fact, I would take mental health days as sick days because some days I just couldn't face going back to my operatory for another day. How do you let your education go by the wayside when you invested so much to have a very specific career?

Taking a look at what was missing, we both felt that we wanted to be our own bosses. We found a side business and worked dental hygiene part-time. The side business, a corporate gift basket company, became all consuming and did not bring in the revenue we required (and hoped for). Prior to purchasing it and after some research, my wife wanted to do it. Normally, I would never agree to get involved in such a business as I did, except I was so happy to have her that I would have agreed to anything she wanted. I personally loathed the side business after a short time. Don't mistake this for blame. I just was not cut out for this business. My wife looked after it, but it was in our home and it still affected me. I'm certain that my lack of interest also affected the bottom line. Then I started having issues with my hand and wrist from practicing dental hygiene. After lots of physical therapy, doctor's appointments, and chiropractic appointments, I had to leave my dental hygiene career. I was unable to practice because of a repetitive strain injury. I had disability insurance, but the insurance company was not cooperative. Again, our finances were spinning out of control. I felt I had failed...again! It felt like I just could not win.

I didn't cope well. I couldn't exercise as I liked, as lifting weights caused further injury to my wrist and hand. I was only a fair-weather runner. I was not a very nice person to be around. I was depressed. I couldn't work and the insurance company made me further demoralized because they wanted to control my working future and were dragging their heels. I drank to cope. I ate to cope. I wasn't contributing and the insurance company wouldn't allow me to work at another vocation. This was not how my life was supposed to turn out. I felt trapped.

A change had to happen. I was demoralized and depressed. My health wasn't great. I was not handling stress well. My chest hurt. I would wake up in the night thinking I was having a heart attack. I had constant pain in my stomach. I felt like I wouldn't be long for this world. Was I too going to have the health issues that my parents had suffered? We were not doing well with our finances. I felt I had no control of my life. I felt like everything that had happened to me had finally overwhelmed me. This was not the life I had envisioned for myself, or my wife. I felt that I must have been such a disappointment to my parents. I often thought, "At least my

Dad didn't have to see what a failure I've become." And, what about my wife? I can't imagine this is what she signed on for. She deserved better. This is not where I thought I would be in my life.

I always envisioned myself with some greater purpose in my life. In everything I had done up to this point, there was something was missing. I wanted to be a great provider for my family and I wanted to make a difference. Neither of which was happening. "Lost" is the best description I can give you to tell you how I felt. How could I make my wife happy if I couldn't even make myself happy?

Then my Mom died.

I had to stop and look inward. As an introvert, I did a lot of reflection. One major point I kept focusing on was whether or not my parents were actually happy all those years following the mantra of get an education and stick with it to the end. In retrospect, I don't remember my Mom and Dad being particularly great with money. I was acutely aware that money was always tight or at least that is how they made it seem. How would I ever get my feet under myself and my family financially stable given the lack of financial education given to me?

I also don't believe my Dad ever truly loved what he did for a living. Even in his retirement, he had to continue working. There had to be more to life than work and be sick and then...nothing.

In some ways I was very much like my Mom and Dad, and in other ways I felt I was a huge disappointment and not like them at all. I was afraid of living a life straining to reach mediocrity, and of illness. Fed up, I started to search for more.

What Now?

The personal history I have shared is part of my story. As I've said before, we all have a story. Mine is not meant to be more remarkable, sad, or happier than anybody else's story. My story is simply for demonstration purposes so you know where I have come from and how I got to where I am now. I hope that, in some way, you might identify with my story and know that there is hope. There is more to life. You can have everything you want in life and more. Some people say you can't have it all. I disagree. I now know that you can have it all. The key is you!

In the following pages, I am going to share some insights with you; insights that I have had to learn on my journey. With this, I hope to make a difference with you, a complete stranger. As you read, you may feel that you need time to pause and reflect. It may take you a few moments or it may take you several days or weeks. That's all right. When you are ready, pick up this book and continue reading from where you left off. The key is for you to really internalize what you are reading and then apply it to your own life. I encourage you to take steps to make change. But please know, it will not always be comfortable. It will take work on your part.

Right now, I want you to commit to the following: **You are worth it!**

No matter where you have come from, how defeated you may feel right now, remember that you are worth it. You are deserving of true happiness. If you take steps to wake up to your beliefs and do what is truly important to you, you will have the ability to transform yourself preparing for your life to flourish and thus attain the wealth and large life you deserve!

"The greatest good you can do for another is not just to share your riches,
but to reveal to him his own."

- Benjamin Disraeli

Wake Up

Chapter 1

Overcome Your Story

"Don't compromise yourself. You are all you've got."

- Janis Joplin

Square Pegs in Round Holes

You have one shot at this life here on earth. You never know when your time might end and you can't control that variable. But, you can control how you treat yourself and make the best of your time while you are here. Some of us have longer than others and some might say that living as old as eighty is a long time, but ask the eighty year old and they might say their life went by like the blink of an eye. I'm sure all of us might think the same thing if we are allowed a moment's reflection at the end regardless of our age. I believe we need to live our life to the fullest. Far too few of us reflect on our lives at the end and realize we lived it well and to the fullest. In fact, I believe that it is a great minority of us that are able to say we lived our destiny on earth. All of us owe it to ourselves to live the richest life possible.

I want you to ask yourself: how have you spent your life to date? This is an important question. If you are dissatisfied in any way, then it is likely time for a change.

Think about our education system. It currently teaches that you must get good grades in school and fit a specific mould in order to be successful in the future. The best way for you to succeed is to then go to a post-secondary institution and further your education in order to get a good job. Again, it involves following the status quo and sometimes trying to fit a square peg into a round hole that just is not going to fit. For several of us, we are that square peg. Please don't get me wrong! I am not, for even a moment, suggesting that getting good grades and furthering your education, is a bad thing. I am saying that this is not the bliss that all of us require. For some, it is, and that is terrific. Some people are the square peg that just won't fit in that round hole. The inability to fit that mould can leave one with a false sense of being worthless than those that do fit the mould. In fact, many people that do forward their education are still not happy. This is something that many square pegs don't realize. It doesn't matter if you have a Ph.D. or a seventh grade education. Regardless, all of us have the same chance at being happy. All of us also have the ability to succeed and live wealthy lives full of happiness. Sadly, many of us won't take the steps to find the answers and live the lives we are truly meant to live.

Many people go through life like a boat in the ocean without a rudder. They let life push them whichever which way and don't seize control. They allow life's experiences and other peoples' ideals to influence them. They are unhappy and merely exist and don't live their own authentic life. All of us have a past. I gave you a good dose of my past in the introduction. Many would read what I wrote earlier and ask, "What is he complaining about?" The point of me writing about my past was to demonstrate that we all come from different upbringings and different experiences. What I wrote isn't complaining or necessarily remarkable when compared to anyone else, but simply an account of some of my past experiences in a nut shell and how my perception of these experiences have affected me, including the assumptions I have made based on those experiences. It is my story. It is what it is and there is nothing I can do to change the past. Your past may not be fireworks and incredible struggles, but like me, I am willing to bet that you are allowing your assumptions about how you think others think you should live your life affect you. Like me, this could be causing great chaos and confusion in your life. You are that boat without a rudder.

It's easy to get hung up on past experiences, as it can be difficult to let go. Perhaps you're angry. Perhaps your past has made you feel limited in your potential as a person. Maybe you made some poor choices and you can't get past them. I have a friend named Jason that married my second wife (I don't like calling her that because she is my one and only and the one I was always meant to love) and myself. He's a minister. I was very honest with him when I caught him up on my past after not seeing him for over ten years. I let him know the struggles I had and how I did things I may not have been proud of. I let him know that I could have been a better husband the first time around and that I drank and partied way too much. He said to me, "I don't care where you've come from, but I care where you're going." Now, I know what my good friend Jason meant by saying that to me, but what a terrific metaphor for life...for all of us. It doesn't matter where you've come from, but where you are going. There is really only one person that can control this direction. That person is you!

When you allow the assumptions you made from your past experiences to rule how you live your life now, you aren't being your authentic self. Yes, you need to learn from experiences, but who says you can't dream and then turn those dreams into a reality? What have you always wanted to do? Many of us have likely heard ourselves say that we always wanted to live in a certain locale, or do a certain career, or travel to certain places. To many people these are pure fantasies because they could "never" do such things. Instead they continue to do what is "expected" of them, even though they know it does not make them truly happy or fulfilled. Where do these expectations come from? They come from our own assumptions and perceptions of our past and the majority of time they are false.

Travel Light

I'm sure all of us have met people that have what they claim is "baggage." The Oxford Dictionary defines baggage as: "Past experiences or long-held attitudes perceived as burdensome encumbrances." Who defines this baggage? Is it other people or you? In all honesty, nobody has a right to judge your past. Who doesn't have a past? What's done is done. It gets tiring carrying all that personal and psychological luggage around. You need to quit torturing yourself. If you are beating yourself up because of the assumptions you have drawn from past experiences, you have to stop.

Again, I want to make a very careful distinction here. **Letting go of your past does not mean disregarding it or forgetting it.** I'll delve into my own personal experience to help you understand better. I made some assumptions from my past that limited my future. While I love my Mom and Dad and would never want any other parents than them, I was always afraid to disappoint them. I let their voices of caution reign over my future experiences. I was always looking for their approval. I needed it. My parents did not necessarily want this to happen, but this was my perception. *I made* these assumptions. I didn't talk about it with them because I didn't want to appear weak and I simply did not have the confidence to truly understand what I was feeling. I was also afraid that I would be like my Mom and Dad financially because that is where I came from and I had no education to understand finances or how to further myself financially. I felt that I would be sick throughout my life and unable to reach my potential. My childhood depression experience left me feeling brittle and unconfident for many years. For a few of my early teenage years I felt like an outcast. My peers didn't understand me and I felt very alone. I didn't enjoy school. I had to work very hard to be a mediocre student. I didn't have any siblings close to me in age that I felt I could approach with what I was going through. All of them were married by the time I was twelve years old. It seemed as though we were on separate planets. I was a little jealous of how they had one another and shared experiences. I failed at marriage, the first in my family to fail at marriage. Serious illness touched my own personal family. Why did that happen? My wife and I struggled with a business that I hated. So what do I do with all of these experiences and the assumptions I made about who I am based on these experiences?

Quite simply I realized I was playing the victim and had been doing so most of my life. The victim is weak and I was tired of being weak. I had to realize that I am not my past. I am not my parents. I am not my siblings. I am not my old friends. I am uniquely me. To void my past would mean to dishonour my parents. It would mean dishonouring my ex-wife. It would mean that I considered a part of my life worthless and I don't want to forget a part of my life that taught me so much. These past experiences and perceptions made me who I am today and part of being successful in life means accepting these "negative" experiences and transforming them into learning opportunities. It means realizing that perceptions and assumptions made are just that, perceptions and assumptions that can so often be false.

What did you learn? My past taught me that I have empathy and love for my family. I know what depression looks like and I have a better idea of what I need to do to look after myself. I don't need to be jealous because this is who *I* am. This is my life and my very own experiences and perceptions and I will choose what shapes my today and my tomorrows. I now like learning because I dictate what I learn and read. I learned how to be a better husband from my first marriage. I know what I don't want to do with my financial situation for my family and myself, and conversely, I know what I want to do financially. I know that if I take care of myself and manage stress that I will be healthy and around for the long run for my wife and our children. I feel blessed now because we went through a serious health scare. It was a wake-up call to live a better life. I learned a lot from owning my first business. I learned the ins and outs of running a business. I learned what I excelled at in business, what I hated, and what I wasn't very good at, which has given me tools to be better prepared for the businesses I now have. I know that I want to be a loving man to my wife and children and that I want my kids to grow up and be their own unique and incredible selves. I know that my family is the single most important thing to me in my life.

Your past experiences will be different from mine. Maybe you blame yourself for something from your past. Understand that nobody is perfect. You need to find it within yourself to grant yourself forgiveness so you can truly put this experience behind you and move on. You still need to go through the same process of evaluation and find what you learned from the experience. If you long for improvement in yourself and for happiness, then you need to let go. If you have done wrong to another and they won't forgive you, then you need to make peace with yourself. To truly turn that transgression around, wouldn't it be a great idea to come out the other end a better person? To become a better human being after wronging another and accepting responsibility is truly learning from an experience. Forgiving yourself doesn't mean you are not accepting responsibility for your actions, but it does mean that you are ready to be better. To be better, you need to forgive number one. Give yourself permission to move on. Look for the positive from the experience. What did you learn? If you find this hard to understand within yourself, reach out for guidance. It's worth it if it gets you to your better self.

Learn from your past, but realize that you aren't your past. In fact, by assessing my past and taking lessons from it, I suddenly realized that I have value and something to contribute to the world. Now why would I ever want to disregard my past when it has taught me so much? I no longer believe in "baggage." I just carry a small carry-on with me through my life journey, just large enough for the positive experiences and lessons from my past. The experience I had with this type of assessment is something anybody can do. It's not something that necessarily happens overnight. It will take time and it can be a very confusing. You will need to process your feelings. Do some quiet reflection and make some notes. Write down all of the positives you can think of from your past. Take the negatives and write down the positive lessons these experiences have taught you. If you can't get the positives from the negatives, then you might need a little more time to think on it, but it is in there. You can turn almost any experience into a positive if you open yourself up to it. Sometimes the positive in the experience is simply learning from the experience. By doing the above you will contribute to your own inner peace. Your past is your past and it is what it is, now leave it in the past.

Accountability

What I mentioned above is about perceptions, but it is also about accountability. As soon as you take responsibility for where you are in your life, you will be ready to move forward to a better you. Realize that you are where you are because of the choices you made, whether good or bad. Forget trying to rationalize why you made the choices you did. Do not blame others for the decisions you made, or for your perceptions. If you are angry, stop being angry. Take a breath and calm your mind. You are to blame. I know that saying that to yourself can hurt, but sometimes, the truth hurts.

It does not matter as to what your circumstances may be, past or present. You played a leading role in your life whether you realized it or not. Were you not an active participant, at least in your own mind? Surprise! You played the leading role and you will continue to play the leading role. Accept what is and realize that you have always been the star of your own life. Accepting responsibility can be extremely liberating once you realize that, to a great degree, you are in control. Understand that being accountable is not about weakness. It gives you power. It is the realization that you are in control!

Being accountable means accepting responsibility for your actions. There is no justification. There are no excuses. You did "a" and "b" occurred. There are no "yeah, buts." Your decisions have led you to where you are right now. It's not your family. It's not your job. It's you! You are the architect for your life.

Being accountable is also about commitment. It's about your follow through. What are you going to do now? The power of true accountability can lead to life changing results full of happiness and success, but it is not the easy road. It is far easier to play the victim than to stand up and follow through with a plan to be better. To be accountable means to do what you say you are going to do. It is the only way you will be better than you are right now.

This is a theme that will continue to come up throughout this book. You play the leading role in your life. The question is, *will you write the script? Are you ready to be accountable?*

Life is Too Short

When you come to your own epiphanies about your past and all of the positives that are now available to you from what you once thought were self-limiting experiences, I hope you understand that life is too short to allow yourself to be ruled by the negative. You are a unique individual with great value and have something to contribute to the world. To further grasp the concept of "unique value," I encourage you to look for the distinctiveness that is in every individual whom you come into contact. Perhaps they are good at their occupation, or it might be their ability to make you feel good about yourself. Everybody has an inherently unique value. Some of us just don't know it yet.

I had a friend that was gravely ill and in the hospital, only having a few weeks of life left on earth. When I went to visit with him, we had a really good chat. In our conversation, he expressed to me how there were so many things that he had always wanted to do, but never did. He talked about how he wished he travelled more; about how he wished he had started his own company years ago instead of working the same job that he never really enjoyed; he wished he had a better relationship with his family; and so on. Later that day, I was overwhelmed by emotion. How many people come to the end of their life as my friend was coming to the end of his life, wishing they had done x, y, and z? What bothered me the most was that my friend did not have to die with any regrets. He could have done it all. He could have travelled more. He could have started his own business and not work in a job that left him dissatisfied. He could have worked towards a better relationship with his family. He could have done all of these things, but for whatever reason, he chose not to proceed.

"**Life is too short**." This is now and forever more, one of my personal mantras that I say to myself often in order to keep my life journey in check. My friends, family and colleagues have also heard me say the same. For me, life is too short to be negative. Life is too short to spend doing a job I don't enjoy. Life is too short to work with people I don't enjoy. Life is too short to spend with people that are negative and bring me down. Life is too short to not look after my health. Life is too short to not spend as much of it as I can with my wife and children. Life is too short to not do some things just for me. Life is too short to be angry, bitter, or unappreciative. Life is too short to not enjoy it. This is how I constantly remind myself of how I want to live my life. It reminds me that I have so many things that I want to enjoy and that I want to do. It has actually made my life a little busier, but in a good way. I work very hard to dictate what I want to do with my life. This includes working on this book, helping people to live their best life, working on my real estate business, working on my other ventures, scheduling time just with me and my son and daughter, scheduling time with just me and my wife, scheduling time to exercise and to read and invest in myself, as well as vacations to spend as a family to places we want to visit and enjoy. This may not be what you want to do with your life and that's fine. To me I am living my best life and, more importantly, loving it!

Take a moment and look at your life. What are you putting off today that you could be missing out on?

A Worthy Ideal

You likely won't change your life simply to change it. You need a good reason to change. You need something that will drive you to be better. By that I mean, a greater reason or motivating factor to become a better you; a successful you however you imagine yourself to be. This is known as a worthy ideal. Another definition would be your values and priorities. Maybe you want to be healthy, to lose some weight and get in shape for the reason that you want to be healthy and around for your family for the long run. The goal is health, but the worthy ideal is to be around for your family. This could be a worthy ideal to some people. Maybe one of your goals is to make more money and then to fund a school for orphans in a poor country. Money is the goal, but the worthy ideal is to make things better for the orphans. You could have many goals that are because of a single worthy ideal. Your worthy ideal may be very different than somebody else's, but it has to speak to something that is very important to you, something that is truly within your heart. Without the worthy ideal, you may reach your goal or goals, but can you sustain your goals? Having a worthy ideal will be your motivating factor. Without careful introspection, you may not realize what your worthy ideal is, or that you have a worthy ideal. Take some time and identify it. Mine are my children and my wife. I want to make my life better and, in turn, make a great life for them. Trust me, this is great motivation for me.

Another motivating factor may be that you want to be a better you for somebody else. That is a terrific worthy ideal. This doesn't mean you are living your life for them, but you want to be a happier and overall healthier person, mentally, physically, and spiritually, whatever that looks like for you. Keep in mind that you can't be better for somebody else until you can be better for yourself. You have to take care of yourself first before you can take care of somebody else. Make sure you take time for yourself because it not only benefits you, but others around you.

You have one shot at this life. Think about it. If you have one shot at something, why would you not want to give it your all? Easy to answer "yes," yet many of us take our lives for granted. We don't look after ourselves. We beat ourselves up. We do things we don't want to do on an ongoing basis. We don't take time to smell the roses or savour the experience of life on a daily basis. We won't be on this earth forever. Our time is limited.

How have things been in your life to date? Is it working for you or is it time to make a change? It may be time to get your house in order and become the rich human being that you are destined to be. I don't necessarily mean rich in the sense of money, but in how you live your life, contribute to society, and reap the happiness that you deserve. Learn from your past, but don't pigeon hole yourself because of it. Because you are human, you can adapt and change and do whatever you want to do with your life. Isn't that beautiful?

> "You are not judged by the height you have risen,
> but from the depth you have climbed."
>
> - Frederick Douglass

> "The longer we dwell on our misfortunes,
> the greater is their power to harm us."
>
> - Voltaire

Chapter 1: Points for Self-Examination

- Don't be a square peg in a round hole.
- Let go of past experiences and your false perceptions.
- You are not a victim!
- Be an active participant in your life.
- Find your true values and priorities.
- Understand what your worthy ideal is.

Chapter 2

Burn and Learn

"To every disadvantage there is a corresponding advantage."

- W. Clement Stone

Success Begins with a Few Failures

All of us have likely felt that we have failed at one time or another. Some of us may feel like we have failed a lot. When you want to succeed and, by definition, success is replaced by failure, it can be incredibly demoralizing. Here is the definition of failure as given in the Oxford Dictionary: "lack of success; the omission of expected or required action." It's pretty negative. I know what it's like to want to succeed and yet to feel like you fail and fail again. It's frustrating. It makes you want to give up.

The truth is that failure can also be defined as an education. Where some people see defeat and envision it as an insurmountable brick wall, successful individuals face it head on and see the lesson in the defeat. They break through that brick wall, and if that isn't possible, then they find other ways to go over, under, or around it. They don't let it slow them down or ruin their resolve.

Successful writers and speakers and those who know success will say to "fail and fail often." The thinking that goes with this statement is that each failure gets you closer to success. This form of thinking has a lot of validity and is way more positive than the Oxford definition. Nobody is perfect even though all of us look at some people and think everything they touch turns to gold. The truth is that to become good at something takes a lot of practice. The results may not be what you want right away. You have to do it over and over again. If at first you don't succeed and you don't try again, then there will be no success. It really is that simple. Imagine when you were a child learning to walk and you fell down. If you never got up again you would have never learned to walk. What if while learning to speak as a child that you gave up completely and never spoke again, not because you couldn't do it, but because you would not try any further? It may seem like a ridiculous example, but it fits the thought process of failing and failing often to find success. As a child you had tenacity. You kept trying and you learned something from each time you did not succeed. You likely had a parent or caregiver cheering you on as you made each effort, praising you every time you simply tried to succeed. It is beneficial to have positive people to help you and cheer you on as you work towards your dreams now.

My own personal experiences speak to not succeeding and not finding my true personal happiness in life until I was a 37, 38, 39, even a 40 year old! This doesn't mean I wasn't good at anything or that I never enjoyed my life up to that point, but I was searching for personal meaning. I wanted to do something with my life that would make me happy and inspire me. My loved ones loved me and felt I was good at what I did. In their eyes I was a contributing member of society. Personally, I wanted more. Knowing this, I changed jobs and careers. I searched to find true love after my first marriage didn't work. I searched to realize that my past will have no bearing on who I am. While I felt quite isolated and alone in my unhappiness at times, I can't imagine having given up. I would be so disappointed because I have now hopped the hurdle and made the leap to my own personal discoveries.

Alcoholics Anonymous says that the first step to recovery is in realizing that you have a problem. This is the exact same for finding your true happiness in life. You can't search for it until you know you want and need it.

Great, now how do you find it? It's going to take some effort and you are going to encounter a few roadblocks, or failures. Remember to burn and learn. Take what you learned from your failures and then put it behind you and move forward.

Successful Failures

The truth of the matter is that you will likely incur a few failures before you encounter success. This is all right and certainly not a negative. You are learning and by doing so you are that much closer to success. Not quite sure what a successful failure can look like? Here are a few examples of people that got knocked down, but got right back up again. You may be surprised by some of the following information. I know I was:

Albert Einstein, arguably one of the greatest scientific and mathematical minds of our times, didn't speak until he was four years old. He was a good student, but daydreamed and many of his teachers thought he was lazy and would never amount to anything. Albert kept up with his daydreaming and invented the theory of relativity (but, please don't ask me to explain it!). His contributions to science have helped shape the world in which we know today. Talk about marching to your own drum and ignoring the negativity from those around him.[1]

Famous comedian and Hollywood A-lister, **Jim Carrey** came from a poor family. For a time he and his family lived on the street. He had a dream of being a comedian and worked his way up from the clubs in Toronto to being the actor his is today. The amount of money he has made in his career to date is staggering. In fact, his entire net worth is now $150 million![1]

Writer **Stephen King** had the manuscript for his first book rejected over thirty times. He was so frustrated that he threw it in the trash only to have his spouse retrieve it and urge him to pursue it further. This book has since been turned into a cult classic not once, but twice, and sold over 1 million copies its first year in publication.

---

[1] Jacques, Renee. 16 Wildly Successful People Who Overcame Huge Obstacles to Get There. *Huffington Post*. TheHuffingtonPost.com, Inc. Sept. 25, 2013. June 11, 2015. http://www.huffingtonpost.com/2013/09/25/successful-people-obstacles_n_3964459.html.

The book? *Carrie*. Today he has had over 350 million copies of his books published. Many of his works have been turned into motion pictures. If you have ever read any of his books, you know he is very good at his craft. Not succeeding over thirty times for most people might mean defeat, but for King, he just forged ahead (with a little push from his wife).[1]

Thomas Edison invented the light bulb. It is estimated that he was unsuccessful in the range of 1,000 to 10,000 attempts. His response to not getting it right was: "I have not failed. I've just found 10,000 ways that won't work." Where would society be today if Mr. Edison had given up?[1]

Charlize Theron is the first South African actress to win an Academy Award and is a highly respected Hollywood actress. As a child she witnessed her mother defend herself against her alcoholic father by fatally shooting him. Instead of being a victim to the trauma she witnessed, she instead became the success that she is today.[1]

Oprah Winfrey is one of the richest people in the world, known for her charities, O Magazine and for her long running daytime television talk show, *Oprah*, and is estimated to be worth over $2.9 billion. She ran away from home as a young teen after being the victim of molestation and had a child at the age of fourteen, who passed away shortly after birth. Ms. Winfrey then excelled in high school as an honours student and won a full scholarship to college before further becoming a television personality. What an incredible story of perseverance and of the triumph of the human spirit![1]

Donald Trump is an icon in business.[2] Almost everybody is familiar with him. Like him or not, he is the epitome of success. Did you know that he had some huge failures? I mean losing almost all

---

[2] Maddalone, Joe. 5 Reasons Everyone Should Follow Donald Trump's Advice. *Forbes*. Forbes.com. March 30, 2012. June 11, 2015. http://www.forbes.com/sites/joemaddalone/2012/03/30/5-

of his net worth to the point of filing for bankruptcy not just once, but FOUR TIMES![3] That is a huge deficit in which to overcome. Many people would give up. Because of his tenacity, he kept trying and succeeded to become the mogul he is today. He is a business magnate and a celebrity with his reality television series: The Apprentice and The Celebrity Apprentice.[4]

All of the above individuals overcame some sort of adversity in order to triumph. Success seemed to be a challenging concept for all of them given past failures, difficult experiences, and/or a lack of belief and support from other individuals. There are countless stories of people not succeeding in order to finally succeed. In fact, I would wager that almost everyone who has succeeded has first gone through many challenges and so called failures. They have failed and failed often, learning each time about the experience, and more importantly, themselves.

3-Minute, 3-Hour, or 3-Day Relationships

As I alluded to earlier, it is easier to recover from a failure and carry on to success if you have the support of somebody that believes in you. Please know that this is not the rule of success, but it does aid in it. Stephen King's wife retrieved his book from the garbage because she believed in him. It's hard to say if all of the above people had the

---

reasons-everyone-show-follow-donald-trumps-advice/.

[3] Bingham, Amy. Donald Trump Files for Bankruptcy Four Times. *ABC News*. ABC News Internet Ventures. April 21, 2011. June 11, 2015. http://abcnews.go.com/Politics/donald-trump-filed-bankruptcy-times/story?id=13419250&singlePage=true.

[4] Wikipedia, the free encyclopedia. The Apprentice (U.S. TV Series). *Wikipedia, The Free Encyclopedia*. Wikimedia Foundation, Inc. June 6, 2015. June 11, 2015. http://en.wikipedia.org/wiki/The_Apprentice_(U.S._TV_series).

same sort of support. Sometimes you have to tune out the negative noise from others in order to find success, just as Einstein was able to ignore his negative teachers early in life.

Jim Rohn, a highly acclaimed entrepreneur, author, and motivational speaker, has said you are the sum of the five individuals that you hang out with and that you assimilate with them. Think about that statement for a moment. Who are the five people whom you spend the most time with whether as a friendship or a business relationship? Examine how they make you feel. Are they positive or are they negative? Do they seem to drain you? It could be possible that these individuals are not the best people for you to spend and give of your time. I'm not purporting that you should get a divorce should you feel your spouse is negative. A good relationship is about communication and support and I hope you have that or can at least portray to your loved one that you need this from them. If your coworkers are negative and always tell you that you can't accomplish what you tell them you want to accomplish, then maybe you need to tune them out. Perhaps you need not trust them with your hopes, dreams, and plans. They are not worthy. Keep them in your work file and don't be influenced by them. It is always a good idea to get to know somebody that is doing what you want to do. Get to know somebody that is positive. In the above example, perhaps it is somebody outside of work.

If your siblings or in-laws or some other person in your family is negative, you can limit your time spent with them for your own mental health. Again, perhaps they are not worthy to be sharing in your ambitions. I'm fortunate that my siblings are pretty positive and supportive. The same goes for your friends. Be careful whom you allow into your inner circle.

Once you recognize the effect your peers have on you, categorize them into groups. There are your three-minute friends, your three-hour friends, and your three-day friends. The better the quality of the person, the bigger the time category for that person. If they are a drain, place them in the three-minute category. Positive, but don't necessarily feed you, these become your three-hour friends. For those where you are supported, gain positivity, and are energized, these individual become your three-day group. This can apply to any and all of your relationships. I had a friend that I really liked, but became draining on me. The constant negativity became too much for me and it was affecting me personally. I am still his friend, but he has since become a three-minute friend.

Think about learning a sport such as tennis. If you don't play with players that are better than you, then your progress will be stagnant or at least progress at a very slow rate. If you play with somebody that is a better player than you, it forces you to up your game. You become better more quickly than if you continued to hang out and play with players that are at your current level. The same goes for relationships. Enrich your life with quality people and you will reap the benefits of those relationships.

I know that I really like to get to know and bounce ideas off of, what I consider to be, successful business people. These are people that I feel are where I want to be or where I want to go. I also like to spend time with people that smile a lot and are just plain positive. I like to spend time with people that have similar interests in terms of family and in terms of self-betterment. I also avoid arrogance as much as I can because if this person is in my group of five, then I don't want to be lumped into the same attitude or worse, have it rub off on me. Remember that the people you associate with, along with their views of the world, rub off on you and help to determine your success, unless you are very good at turning off anything negative.

Find Positive Influences

Maybe you're an introvert like me. Maybe your five people looks more like two. That's okay. There are other outlets to help inspire and motivate you to great successes. I have learned so much from motivational books. The pages come alive and allow you to voraciously fill your mind full of information. Some of the information may be repetitive, but it is always a good reminder and there could always be one little tidbit of information that you never knew before. Many of the writers of these books have come from the same place that you and I come from and want the same things. It's always much easier to hear how somebody else got to where you want to go in your life than through trial and error alone. You can also read biographies and other books of interest. But, I recommend being very careful what you read, as you don't want to fill your mind with negative garbage. Choose positive and motivational material that will inspire you to want to reach your goals.

This also goes for television. I did a little experiment a few months back where I stopped watching the news. I noticed that it improved my demeanour to that of one which is more upbeat and positive. Why? The news tends to focus on sad stories and if you watch the news several times a day then you are receiving a lot of negative data on an ongoing basis. If you are afraid that you will miss something important then perhaps only watch it a couple of times a week. You will likely still remain an informed citizen. Another way to keep up without the negativity is to quickly scout the headlines on-line. If something interests you, then read it, but only at your own choosing. Music is the same. The radio also broadcasts a lot of negative news, so try and listen to upbeat music on your iPhone and plug it into your car stereo. Alternatively, you can listen to CD's or podcasts with interviews of interest, but always positive and on a subject that there is something you can learn.

I think you get the idea that you have to be careful of influences. That means people, books, television, and the list goes on. Your mind operates on two levels, the subconscious and the conscious mind. Your subconscious is always operating quietly in the back of your conscious mind. What our conscious mind accepts becomes part of your subconscious mind. The more negativity you allow into your mind, the higher the likelihood that your conscious mind will accept it and it will become a part of your subconscious. Why is this bad? Because your subconscious creates your thoughts and your thoughts lead to actions. Fill your conscious mind with positive influences and be prepared to reap the rewards! When I learned and understood this concept, I had a true "aha!" moment. It really was the beginning of a metamorphosis into who I wanted to be.

Don't mistake what I have said above meaning that you won't drop the ball. You will, but you will take the negativity and change it to a positive. You will learn from the experience. You will get back up and try again and again. Keep filling your mind with positive influences and you will eventually succeed. Perhaps that is how Stephen King kept going after 30 rejections of his first book, or how Thomas Edison persevered with inventing the light bulb.

Bye-Bye, Failure

I dislike the word fail. If you fill your mind with positive influences, you can discard the word fail all together and change it out for the word *experience*. I also mentioned earlier that you could consider failure to equal an education. Either way, there is nothing wrong with experience that educates you. Every experience can be an education. Before I started filling my mind with positive influences, I would look back on my past and think it was negative. How could I ever take anything positive out of my past with a negative attitude and influence on my mind? It's difficult and not very likely. Now, by filling my mind with the positive I am able to easily find the positive.

By putting the positive in, you negate the negative. This certainly applies, and will help you in regards, to what I spoke about in the last chapter.

Filling your mind with the positive has far reaching consequences. You will start to be more positive. People will look at you in a different light because you react differently to situations than they would have predicted. I get a bit of a kick out of when somebody brings something to my attention that they think will really upset me and they themselves are upset and prepared for me to be the same. You start to think differently. Did anybody die? Is anybody hurt? Okay, let's see what we can take from this experience and move on. What may have once been a mountain of obstacles in the past is now considered a molehill or speed bump in comparison.

While you are feeding your mind, you should really take care of the rest of your person. Transforming your mind and the way you think and perceive a so-called negative situation is an incredibly remarkable accomplishment. Make some positives out of other facets of your being. For instance, eat better or eat less. My wife and I started juicing and I love it. I far prefer drinking vegetables as opposed to eating them and I get far more into my person by juicing. Exercise in some kind of capacity at least three times a week. I know it can be difficult to find the time, but make it a priority. I have a Bowflex machine and an exercise bike at home and I run in nice weather (remember – I am only a fair weather runner). I literally schedule it into my day. It helps me to feel better and to feel more confident in myself. Most importantly, is the fact that it is a terrific stress reliever. I also get to set an example for my son, which is a side effect of looking after myself. You have likely heard that the body is the temple. Remember, it is the only body you get here on earth. Positives beget more positives: mind, body, and influencing others. The list goes on.

So far we've explored the idea of looking for the positives in your past and perceived negative situations. We've explored different ways to look at failure and to find the positive in those experiences, and have been exposed to some significant people who have overcome some negative experiences or failure in their lives. We have looked at how the mind works and the importance of filling your mind with positive influences and positive information. We have also looked at other ways to look after yourself and the far-reaching consequences in which the positive can have on others. You may be seeing a trend here.

> "Ever tried.
> Ever failed.
> No matter.
> Try again.
> Fail again.
> Fail better."
>
> - Samuel Beckett

> "What we call failure is not the falling down, but the staying down."
>
> - Mary Pickford

Chapter 2: Points for Self-Examination

- **Fail and fail often.**
- **Seek the positive in all things!**
- **Positive thoughts lead to actions.**
- **Consider failures or negative happenings in your life simply as experiences.**
- **Add positives to your mind and body.**

Chapter 3

Don't Worry; Be Happy

"If a problem is fixable, if a situation is such that you can do something about it, then there is no need to worry. If it's not fixable, then there is no help in worrying. There is no benefit in worrying whatsoever."

- Dalai Lama XIV

What is Worry and Fear?

Worry and fear are some of the most detrimental and unproductive emotions in the world today. One generally leads to the other. Many people live their lives with these emotions at the forefront of their consciousness. They indulge worry and fear as a precursor to a future event. That's right. Living with regards to something that has not yet happened. By doing so they are trying to predict their future.

Worry and fear are used as tools for manipulation. We do it to ourselves, sometimes unwittingly, and people use these emotions on others in order to control them, to have them cow to them. It can lead to other negative feelings like guilt. It can lead to procrastination and ultimately inaction.

Nations use worry and fear to justify their actions to the electorate. They justify the need for war based on fear of what an opposing nation might do. The population worries that this prophesied action might actually happen and so, because of this worry, they fear the worst and the action is suddenly justified. Think of the invasion of Iraq. The fear was that Saddam Hussein had weapons of mass destruction waiting for action. The populace began to worry given the propaganda and therefore the government felt it was justified to invade Iraq. No weapons of mass destruction were ever found.

It can be challenging to shift your focus away from worry and fear. Society often operates using these emotions. The law, while consequence based, can create these emotions. People fear the consequence, so they uphold the law. Religion can operate in the same way. If you sin and don't repent, you are going to Hell.

Take a moment and examine why you worry and what you fear. Perhaps it's Sunday and you're worried about the workload that awaits you at work on Monday morning. Monday hasn't even arrived yet. Maybe you fear screwing up the presentation you need to give to your co-workers, even though you are prepared and know the material inside and out. Worrying about it is not bringing anything useful to you.

These are the very same emotions that impede people from making true change in their lives. They worry about what the future might look like. They fear making change because they are afraid that things might not be at least as good as they are right now. This constant state of worry and fear is useless. How can anybody know what the future will hold? It simply cannot be done. What people can do is to make a good plan and create goals that focus on their values and then do the daily work, the small improvements, to create positive change.

In his book, *The Power of Now - A Guide to Spiritual Enlightenment*, Eckart Tolle says that problems are illusions. Problems, like worry and fear, are manifestations of the future. In fact, many people have their entire identity as revolving around worry and fear. Cut out the future and the past. Think about right now, this very moment. Do you have any problems; any worry or fear at this very moment? The honest answer is no. Right now you are reading. You have no reason to worry or fear. Again, the thought that worry and fear are manifestations of the future holds true. My point is that everybody has some sort of worry and fear within their life. The question is how will you handle worry and fear?

The Broken Clock

Many people come by worry and fear as a product that is handed down to them from their parents or caregivers. My own well-meaning parents implanted these emotions into me. You may know what I'm talking about. "You can't go there, it's too expensive. You can't do that, you might get hurt. You can't do that, it's too difficult. You can't try that, you won't like it." Worry and fear are the emotions being conveyed to predict the future. They are a defence mechanism. In truth, parents rarely knowingly want to hold their children back. It's simply their way of protecting their children, not wanting anything bad to happen to you. And while, short term, this may seem like "loving" emotions, they are more detrimental in the long term.

Think back in your own life. Be honest with yourself. How many times have you been worried or fearful about certain future happenings only to find out that there was no reason to worry or to be fearful? I would bet that it was often. I also believe that the actual act of being worried and fearful was very stressful to you. We've all done it. You are relieved to find out you were wrong about your worry and fear. In your relief, you may have felt like the lead up to the event took years off of your life. The truth of the matter is that the things that we worry about or are fearful of are generally figments of our own imagination.

You might be saying that sometimes it is all right to be worried and fearful, that it was justified. Yes, that sometimes happens, but the vast majority of time it is not justified. Out of 86,400 seconds in a day, a broken clock is right twice. That's not a terrific track record. Pessimists like to dwell on worry and fear in the off chance that they might be right some of the time, just like the broken clock. When you attract the negativity that you put out to the world you might be right a little more often than the clock. But, if you think about the physical damage you are doing to yourself without even knowing it because of the stress of being worried and fearful, it is not worth it and I urge you to do your best to greatly reduce these emotions in your own life. You will notice that when you reduce these emotions, you will become a bit more liberated. Liberated in your physical, emotional, and mental well being. You set yourself up to create positive changes, changing the self-fulfilling prophecy of negativity to positive outcomes.

Elimination

If you are getting what you are putting out into the world, then you are attracting worry and fear. Shawn Achor says it best in his book, *Before Happiness*. He discusses the need to cancel out thought patterns that lead to a negative reality by emitting three opposing waves of positive energy. They are:

> **Wave 1:** I will keep my worry in proportion to the likelihood of the event.
>
> **Wave 2:** I will not ruin ten thousand days to be right on a handful.
>
> **Wave 3:** I will not equate worrying with being loving or responsible.

When put it in this kind of perspective, one can really see how wasteful it is to give in to worry and fear. Achor also has two tips to help protect you from the self-fulfilling nature of negative prophecies:

1. How often has this negative event happened to me in the past?

2. How often does this negative event happen to people in my situation?

Not only is worry detrimental to you as a person, think of the influence it has on your relationships with other people. Recall the last few times you encountered a worrywart. Did you enjoy being with that person or did you feel drained after being around them? The saying "misery loves company" is a fitting quote in terms of what worry warts want from you. They want to be validated in their worry and fear. Often times it may seem like any positive or uplifting responses you provide are down played and refuted with more worry and fear. I'm sure none of us want to spend a lot of time with that worrywart or be that person.

Worry and fear in the workplace is counterproductive to obtaining results. I know that in my business life I don't want to hear worry and fear from those on my team. I understand genuine concern or questions for clarity sake. Instead of worry and fear - I consider roadblocks people put in place to be worried and fearful - I prefer to hear alternate approaches to an issue or a challenge. It is far more productive. Something my father used to say in his professional career as a school principal was, "If you're not part of the solution, you're part of the problem." Worry and fear are the complete opposite of being productive. In other words, they're the problem.

Parents, and I'm speaking to myself here as well, please don't utilize worry and fear towards your children and then say it's because you love them or because you want the best for them. Of course, don't let little Ricky jump off the railing of the ferryboat. That is not what I'm talking about and I'm not talking about eliminating rules put in place to protect your children. It's more about considering your words before you speak to your kids about what they dream about and want to accomplish. Don't be the voice in their back pocket that holds them back as they proceed through life.

Consider how worry and fear affects your spouse or significant other. It's almost the same as speaking to your children. Instead of being worried about what your spouse wants to accomplish and putting up road blocks because of your own worry and fear, offer to talk things out and figure out how to make things come to fruition. With proper planning there is no need to fear the results of the outcome. This way you won't be the wet blanket that is resented over time. The communication will also go a long way to forging stronger bonds between the two of you.

Now consider what role worry and fear plays in your own life. Are you trying to predict a negative outcome before it happens? Are you putting up roadblocks to your own success because you fear not being successful? Do worry and fear create your identity? These same emotions often cause procrastination towards your goals. Realize that planting these seeds of doubt may cause you to harvest the failure you are predicting. Concentrate on all the things that you want to go right. Don't be that person that rains on the parade whether it is your own plans or that of somebody else. A true, loving demeanour towards yourself and others is one in which you nurture the possibilities. By responsibly focusing on the positives instead of fear and worry, you can eliminate negative outcomes.

Feel It and Call It Out

Listen to your body. Emotions such as worry and fear manifest themselves, not only in thought, but also in a physical sense. They are stressful emotions. It's all right to experience worry and fear. As I mentioned, everybody is worried and fearful at one time or another. It's now about managing worry and fear.

In dealing with a problem you can remove yourself from the situation, deal with it, or accept it. You can cope with worry and fear in the same way. An example is something that happened to me the other day. I received a phone call about an outstanding invoice that I was certain I had already paid over a year ago. That was it, but I was worried and fearful about having to deal with combing through my files to see if I did actually pay it and then have to return the phone call from the company looking for their money. It was incredibly minor in nature, but I could feel the nervousness building within me, mainly because I dislike dealing with anything to do with accounting. The tension was building in me and I had to slow down and recognize what I was feeling and why I was feeling it. I didn't like it. It was casting a terrible funk on my morning. I then had to accept what might be the worst thing that could happen in the situation, and whether or not this "worst thing" would be the end of the world. (Hint: No...it wouldn't) The worst case scenario would be that I did not pay the invoice and would have to pay it. After I accepted this possible fact, I actually felt better. In the end it turned out that I didn't pay the original invoice. I could not find it in my accounting files and had to pay it. Nobody died and I felt so much better after I dealt with it. This is an example of just how ridiculous it can be to be worried and / or fearful. In this scenario I chose to deal with it. I accepted full responsibility for and, in the end, I felt much better.

If you can quiet your mind and pay attention to how you feel both mentally and physically, you can better understand when fear and worry are acting upon you. By recognizing it you are actually calling it out, so to speak. "Hey, I see you!" Now punt it from your conscious and self-conscious mind. I know this may seem easier said than done. Face the worry and fear head on. What is the worst that could happen? Would it be the end of the world? What can you do to ensure that your fear does not happen? By answering these questions you have addressed the issue and you will not just feel better, but be better equipped to handle the situation.

Once you can recognize when worry and fear start to creep into your own subconscious, you can better pay attention to whether or not you put it out to other people. Do you utilize it as a tool to get what you want from others? If so, these individuals may eventually resent you for it. The utilization of fear and worry upon others is passive aggressive in nature. Recognize it and stop it immediately. Pay particular attention to how you talk to your children, spouse / partner, or your staff. Don't hold them back because of how you speak to them. If you want to eliminate worry and fear from you as a person, then you can't utilize it upon others, otherwise you will never cleanse yourself from these negative emotions.

Once you understand and recognize when worry and fear pop up, you will recognize when people try to use it on you to get their way. It can make you angry, but I urge you not to react in such a way. Rather, ask the person if they are trying to make you feel guilty, to make you worried or fearful. This usually makes people stop in their tracks as they realize, often to their own embarrassment, that yes, they are trying to make you feel such a way. Remember that when worry and fear are directed towards another, it is not so much about the person it is directed towards, but more about the person who is directing it. It is about their agenda.

Plain and simple, you need not be worried or fearful. It is what it is, and will be what it will be. Eliminate fear and worry from your life and respond to life's happenings appropriately. Plan for the future, but live in the now!

"Do not anticipate trouble, or worry about what may never happen.
Keep in the sunlight."

- Benjamin Franklin

"I am an old man and have known a great many troubles, but most of them
have never happened."

- Mark Twain

Chapter 3: Points for Self-Examination

- **Realize that worry and fear are detrimental to you and others.**
- **Listen to your body. It can tell you when you are worried and fearful.**
- **Don't allow worry and fear into your subconscious. Eliminate them completely from your conscious mind.**
- **Learn to manage your worry and fear.**

Chapter 4

Social Impact

"Be courteous to all, but intimate with few,
and let those few be well tried before you give them your confidence."

- George Washington

Perceptions of Relationships

We've already discussed the need to have positive people and positive influences in your life, but will go into these topics in a little more depth here. It's important to be able to identify those that truly influence you whether right now or in your past. Sometimes our own perceptions about what others think hold us back. It's also important to recognize if there are people in your life that hold this type of influence over you, whether in the past or the present. It's important to recognize if it is a positive or a negative influence, and if it is your own perception of the relationship that may be adversely affecting you.

Let me explain using my own past and my own perceptions. I have tremendous love and respect for my parents. I also recognize now that I cared what they thought of my choices and, consequently, myself. I think that I cared so much that it was to my detriment. I wanted to make them proud. If I screwed up, I beat myself up because of how much I felt I had disappointed my Mom and Dad. Now I'm not so sure if my parents would have really cared if I had gone out, swung for the fences and failed, but I certainly perceived that this was the case.

As I mentioned in the intro, in 2007, when my wife and I were going through a yearlong life and death health scare, my father passed away. Anyone that has lost a parent knows it is a difficult time. I felt bad that I could not be by his bedside when he passed as some of my brothers and sisters were able to do, but I think that my Dad knew I needed to be with my wife. I was genuinely shook up at losing a man that meant so much to me and held so much influence over me. He never made any bones about being the patriarch of the family and I think he knew he had some influence.

After a few months passed and after things started looking up for my wife and I, we had decided that life was too short not to live our lives to the fullest. This is when we decided we wanted to go into business for ourselves. It was the beginning of what I would later consider a failed business venture for us (now considered a learning business venture). It became another stressful time and the way I dealt with that stress and later the stress of everything that had built up, including losing my Dad, not enjoying the business and not being able to do my day job due to injury, was less than stellar. In a way I was a little lost without my Dad. Perhaps if he hadn't died I would have dealt with all of my stresses in a more positive manner. I drank and I didn't exercise. I was a bear to be around and moped. After a while it occurred to me that I didn't have to please my Dad. My Dad was gone and he had no more cares for the earthly world. I was no longer responsible, in my own perception, to him. To be frank, it was a little bit freeing. Why was I beating myself up?

My Mom was still alive and I cared a great deal about her. However, a couple years after my father's passing, her health started to fail. In 2010, I was making strides to finding my true "me," but I was still a ways away. It was then that she died after a very difficult illness. I was with her for several days before she passed and returned to my home a few hours before she left the world. In that time with her I had the opportunity to tell her how much I loved her. My wife was pregnant with our first child and I told her how I wanted to be a great parent to my son. My mother's love for me was a very protective love. I was glad that she would not suffer anymore as she had suffered in the final months of her life.

I took some time to mourn and heal from my last surviving parent leaving the world. After some reflection, this too became freeing. I almost feel guilty saying such a thing about losing my Mom and Dad. I almost feel like a bad son. Almost. Trust me, I would far prefer to have them here, but this just was not meant to be. I had nobody else that I was truly afraid to disappoint. My wife understands me and wants me to be happy. I know that she is on board with whatever

I choose to do. I could now go out and swing for the fences and take my lumps good or bad and feel less concerned about not doing as my folks had wanted for me. Again, this is, or at least was, my perception. This could very well be the opposite of what my parents wanted for me. To me, I no longer had to play it safe. I didn't have to beat myself up if I thought I didn't impress them. By having this release I became better able to excel.

I am telling you this personal tale because I don't want you to have to go through the same experience if you don't have to.

Perception, right or wrong, can be a powerful thing.

I wish I had cared a little less about the perception I had about how I thought my parents perceived me. If I had, I may have been further ahead earlier in life and able to enjoy the fruits of my labours with my parents before they passed. But, it is our stories that shape and guide us. Earlier I mentioned that sometimes it is okay to be selfish. Don't be held back when it comes to living your life. If you have a relationship with somebody that is similar to mine with my parents, recognize it for what it is, and then take control. Live for you. You have one shot at this life, so live ***your*** life!

Autocratic or Democratic

Brian Tracy, on his CD set, *The Psychology of Achievement*, speaks about parenting styles that influence a child's development and the relationships that these same individuals form as adults. According to Tracy, studies have found that children that are raised in a very strict environment where the leadership in the home is autocratic and the rest of the family just goes along are typically less creative. They have strained relationships with others because they are always striving to please instead of being on a level playing field within the relationship. These same people will often take a similar leadership position when the opportunity arises, which further strains their interpersonal relationships.

He goes on further to state that the same studies have found that children raised in very democratic households, where they are involved in decision making and are asked for their opinion, are more outgoing individuals. They are very social and creative and they play well with others. They are more likely to rise socially, as well in the workplace to management positions.

This is interesting because, although autocratic family leadership structures can still be found today, they are a more rare than they used to be. Is it any wonder that some people wield this autocratic leadership style and clash with others? I have heard of some employers, clearly wielding the autocratic leadership style, complaining about the younger generation, when really it could be a clash between the individuals being raised in an autocratic household and those raised in a democratic household.

As a parent, it is worth noting how we govern our households. I think all of us want to give our children the best chances at success as possible. It truly does start at home. Likewise, it is worth examining where you came from in terms of the leadership style in your home as you grew up. Knowing is half the battle. Again, you don't have to be pigeonholed because of your past. If you exude some of the traits of the individuals raised in autocratic households, then recognize the traits in yourself and make the effort to go above and beyond. You don't have to let your past affect your present and future relationships!

Confidence in You

I believe that living my life concerned about what my parents thought of me comes down to a lack of confidence in myself. This is why I keep saying *my perception* rather than what my parents thought or did. Get ready for this: it has nothing to do with my parents. They are innocent of controlling my life. I will not pin my experiences on my parents and their influence. I've said it already and I'll say it again: I had terrific parents. Have you ever heard the saying, "I can't be responsible for somebody else's feelings?" The other person, not you, owns those feelings. I was responsible for my own feelings and perceptions, not my parents. The realization here? The sooner you take responsibility for you and prepare yourself to move onto a better you, the sooner you will be truly happy and feel more fulfilled. You are in control. Now take control. It comes down to accountability. Be accountable.

I will give you another example as it compares to work. This one partially involves me, but also my past co-workers. As I stated earlier, prior to running my own business, I worked for someone else. Initially I liked my employer, but, over time, he became bitter and began treating his staff with this same attitude. He was passive aggressive, a poor communicator, and made people feel very badly about themselves. I recognized that the situation was not going to improve. Yes, this was my place of employment, but I could get employment elsewhere. I didn't need to be controlled or influenced by this person that truly had issues about himself and his life's circumstances. I didn't need his negativity on me every day. So, I left. I didn't feel the slightest bit bad about it. I happen to really like this person outside of the work environment, but I don't need that negativity in my work life. After all, we spend most of our lives at work and should spend it in an environment that doesn't belittle or make you feel less than you truly are. It's draining and will eventually take a toll on your personal life. Leaving a negative situation was the beginning of taking back control.

What's interesting is that I have some co-workers that still work there. Many of them complain about their jobs, how the boss is demeaning, how he is disrespectful and unappreciative. I ask them when they will find another place of employment. They have been so emotionally beat up and berated that they don't think they are of enough worth to work anywhere else. They have this negative influence over them every day, which carries into all other aspects of their life making them and those around them miserable, and yet, they won't recognize that there is happiness by working somewhere else. If they were truly bad employees they would be fired, but instead they are kept because they can be controlled. They stay because they are not confident enough in themselves to control their own fate.

My experience with my parents was a perceived influence. The experience that I had, and the experience my former co-workers have with their employer, is an actual negative influence, not perceived. Which has proven to be more difficult, for most, to recognize? This situation highlights that actual influence is harder to recognize. Funny, but you would think that the perceived influence is more difficult to recognize. It really comes down to who you are, the level of confidence you have, and whether or not you are ready for change. Are you working on your own happiness? Are you becoming more confident as a result of filling your mind with the positive? Are you truly ready for change; ready to move away from negativity and towards a positive you?

Positive Relationships

Relationships are about give and take. While it is important to recognize a relationship that may hold you back, or a perceived relationship that holds you back, it is also important to recognize positive relationships with people. You need to nurture relationships that are positive and symbiotic in nature. I like to associate with people that I admire, people that I hold in high esteem, people that are happy and positive in nature, and people that I feel are achievers and have the same hunger for success in all parts of their life as I do, whatever they define as success for themselves. I find that I can often find all these traits in the same individual(s). I like to ask questions, listen, and laugh with them. I am always a little taken aback and tremendously honoured when somebody that I hold in high regard asks me for my advice. This is how I know that the relationship truly is symbiotic. It also makes me feel good to know that I have something to offer such a person. There is a mutual respect and this is a healthy relationship. Such associations can offer counsel when advice is needed, whether in business or personal life. The key to these relationships is that there is no hidden agenda.

A good way to recognize such positive figures in your life is to ask yourself who gives without expecting to receive anything in return. I don't necessarily mean giving money to you or to charity, but in general. Who makes you feel better after you spend time with them? Who offers you good advice when you ask for it? Who is achieving or is doing what you want to do on some level? These are terrific people to have and keep in your life. Always be grateful for their friendship and tell them as much. You get what you put out to the world. Being your best self will attract the same people to you.

Raising the Bar

Successful people often have coaches. There are all sorts of coaching relationships. These paid consultants help keep you on the right track and offer you the counsel and guidance you require. There are business coaches, life coaches, fitness coaches, wellness coaches, and the list goes on.

To make sure that you raise your bar, don't hire just any coach. You may need to interview a few of them before you find a fit for you. Hire one that will address the issues for which you need help and challenge you to be more. I find that I do well with a coach that I respect, one that has succeeded, and one that practices what they preach. These types of relationships are more one-sided because they are all about you. Personally, I use a business coach. The sessions are a great way for me to bounce the business ideas I have off of somebody that has succeeded. It's a great way for me to keep going in a positive direction and to help keep me focused. I'm sure my coach would also say that we are friends.

If you can't afford a coach then you can find counsel from others. Perhaps there is somebody you admire, but you aren't really friends. Schedule a lunch and get to know them. Pick their brain for ideas. Form a bond. Another way is to get a group of people together to form a mastermind group. This is a group of individuals that offer counsel to one another for various issues and each member has an equal time for assistance and the opportunity to offer advice if needed. Remember to focus on the positive. AND remember, you have just as much to offer as everyone else because of your own unique story and insights.

Perhaps you have negative family members that drag you down. Since they are your family, it's not as easy to remove this negativity from your life. What can you do? You don't have to ostracize them, but perhaps limit your time with them. Recognition of the situation is half the battle. Remember, they may not get your dreams, so don't share your great potential if they're not worthy and supportive. You can't pick your family, but you can pick your friends and support system. Choose wisely.

I have an amazing friend that has been in my life for over 20 years. He isn't wealthy in the monetary sense, but he is rich in life experience. He lives within his means and he doesn't have more than he needs. He is well travelled and has a terrific gift of gab. People are drawn to him. He is honest. He questions and analyzes things and makes me do the same. He is a positive person. He is thirteen years my senior and I value his unconditional friendship and love. He has seen me at my lowest and has celebrated my triumphs with me.

I tell him my future plans and my dreams and he says he knows I'll do it. He is what I consider an integral part of my family. Early in our relationship he did something amazing for me. He put in a good word for me with a future employer and urged others to do the same, all attaching their business cards to my resume. I really needed this job at the time. I did get the job and I was so thankful and moved that somebody I just met would do this terrific thing for me. I asked him what I could do for him in return and his words still ring in my head today. He said, "Just do something special for somebody else when they most need it." He told me to pay it forward. He is the epitome of the kind of friends I want in my life. What a terrific influence to have in my life. Is there someone you see this potential in?

Be critical about the influences and the people in your life. Are they positive? Are you better for knowing them? Does their influence encourage you to be your best and to move forward to be even better? You deserve to be your best you and the world needs you at your best. Don't be held back. As you continue to work on yourself, you will become more aware of things you previously could neither see nor understand. Teachers will appear when you are ready to be taught and you will be open to the lessons that are presented to you. I will also warn that as you grow into your best you, you may see friends leave your circle. This isn't because of anything you did, but simply because you are attracting individuals to you who will help you step up to who you're meant to be.

Situational Awareness

Another area of influence to consider has to do with the situations in which you place yourself. Growth is about change. Sometimes the situations we put ourselves in will accidentally sabotage this growth. It's important to recognize the situations that may be influencing your lack of progress towards your goals and then change those situations or eliminate them all together. I call this skill situational awareness. To relate a silly example, remember Wile E. Coyote in the Bugs Bunny Road Runner Show? Every time that coyote went after the roadrunner, bad things would happen. Countless times the coyote was blown up or had an anvil land on his head. Clearly, anytime the roadrunner was around him, it sabotaged any and all of his goals, whatever they were. He would be better off avoiding the roadrunner all together.

Life can be a lot like that coyote and roadrunner relationship. If you're not paying attention, as so many people don't in life, you may be sabotaging your very own progress and not even realize it. This is a good time to do the "out of body" exercise that my own coach had me do. Pretend you are outside of your body, looking down at yourself in various situations throughout your day. What are the situations that you mindlessly place yourself into that are holding you back or even making you regress in the pursuit of your goals? Do you need to do a better job of exercising your own situational awareness?

An example would be a person that wants to quit smoking and knows that when they have a drink they want to smoke. A part of their personal culture may be that they often hang out at the pub, shooting pool, and playing darts while nursing a few drinks. Because this behaviour is a stimulant for this person to smoke, they do the very behaviour they want to stop. By putting themselves in the situation where there is alcohol and they partake, they sabotage the goal of quitting smoking.

On a personal level, I know that when I have an alcoholic beverage later at night I often make the bad decision of snacking. It's a bad decision because I am trying my best to watch my waste-line. Every now and again isn't so bad, but I try not to fall into that trap. I know that having a drink will sabotage my weight loss goals, so I change my behaviour. I make a change by not putting myself into that situation in the first place. I avoid having a nightcap all together. I am exercising situational awareness.

I know an individual that wants to increase his financial position and is very career driven. Whenever he gets upset with somebody in a business relationship, his inclination is to cause the other individual hurt by spending money on threatening a lawsuit. The so-called lawsuit may have no grounds and may be completely frivolous, but he does this often and at a personal cost to himself. Surely, this impedes his financial goals in the end. It is also giving him a negative reputation. In fact, he complains about spending money and how he needs to make more money. His own behaviour is sabotaging his goal of making and holding onto his money, not to mention the wasted and negative energy expended on inflicting hurt. He would be better off by taking some time and thinking through his emotions before launching his campaign of revenge. He reacts instead of responding to a situation. This is a great example of putting one's self in a situation that sabotages personal goals. He is not exercising true situational awareness.

Don't put yourself in situations that hinder or block the attainment of your goals. Remember what is important to you. You are a unique and talented individual and you owe it to yourself to shine as brightly as you can and to attain all that you rightfully have coming to you because of your efforts.

> "You cannot give people what they are incapable of receiving."
>
> - Agatha Christie

> "All things are subject to interpretation. Whichever interpretation prevails at a given time is a function of power and not truth."
>
> - Friedrich Nietzsche

Chapter 4: Points for Self-Examination

- **Perceptions of relationships, past and present, can hold you back.**
- **Recognize if you were raised in an autocratic or democratic household.**
- **Build your confidence level in order to affect change.**
- **Seek positive relationships.**
- **Recognize chronic situations that sabotage your personal growth.**

Transform

Chapter 5

Empower

Your Words.
Keep your words positive
Because your words become your behaviour.
Keep your behaviour positive
Because your behaviour becomes your habits.
Keep your habits positive
Because your habits become your values.
Keep your values positive
Because your values become your destiny.

- Mahatma Gandhi

The Most Important Person in the World

Sometimes it can be difficult to put yourself first when you don't hold yourself in very high regard. Perhaps you do nothing but put others first instead of yourself. Let me tell you right now that sometimes it is simply all right to be selfish.

When I ask groups of people who is the most important person in their life, I often get responses like, "my spouse," or "my kids." That's a lie! While these people are incredibly important to you, the most important person in your life is you. You have to be. If you think about it, you will know that this is correct. It is detrimental to you as a person to not look after yourself, to not do things just for you. Remember when I told you that you can't help others until you first help yourself? This falls into that category. You must be a great you for you in order to be a true help to others. Even after you get yourself "right," you still need to take time to recharge and constantly feed yourself daily with things that are important to you in order to maintain your personal happiness. In this chapter, I will touch on a few things that are important to focus yourself on you and lift you to your next level.

Internal Dialogue

Maybe your mother used to say this to you as you grew up. I know my Mom used to. "If you can't say anything nice, don't say it at all." This is a great lesson in which to apply to your social relationships, whether personal or professional. Did you know that for every negative comment you give to somebody else, or that is given to you, that it takes roughly three to five positive comments to nullify the negative remark? For whatever reason, we internalize the negative that is said to us. The bombardment of such statements, whether true or not, can filter through your conscious mind into your subconscious mind. So yes, it is important to build others up and to be positive and hopefully you will receive the same in return. But how are you speaking to yourself? Do you apply the same lesson learned from good old mom to yourself? If you're not, you should!

You need to watch your internal dialogue. Have you ever heard that you are your own worst critic? Berating yourself is not beneficial to you as a person. Yes, we all make mistakes, but it goes back to not dwelling on the negative. Beating yourself up with your internal dialogue also filters through your conscious mind into your subconscious mind. It's not just from external stimuli. Thoughts become actions and if you think poorly of yourself, well, guess what? Why should anybody think any better of you? It doesn't just apply to conscious thinking. Driving down the road and you flippantly call yourself an idiot because you forgot to take out the garbage, a part of you then believes that you are an idiot. You need to speak to yourself in a polite and positive manner. Give yourself a break. You should be your biggest cheerleader.

Speak to the Positive

This practice applies to all things. What you think about and dwell on will manifest itself. All of us have challenges in our lives. Perhaps you are in great financial debt. Don't think about the need to pay back all of the money. Think about all the ways you are going to make money and make it so. Dwelling on debt is a negative practice and doing so may make you go further into debt. Thinking about *how* you will *make* money is positive. The side effect of making money is the act of paying off debt. Do you see the difference? It's subtle, but it's there. Maybe you have a strong family history of health issues and you are afraid that they will manifest in you. By dwelling on this negativity you might make it so. Turn it around. Think about your healthy lifestyle. Take steps to live a healthier lifestyle and your concentration on this positivity will manifest in you. You will be healthy. Put the negative out of your mind.

If this is a difficult exercise for you then I would suggest that you write something down, something positive about the changes you want in your life and how you feel empowered to be making those changes. I recommend a short paragraph that includes your personal life, such as family and health, and business – what you want to do, perhaps even vacations, whatever you want. Write it in the present as though you have already accomplished your goals and repeat it several times a day. You won't have to do this for perpetuity, but a month for sure and maybe longer. It helps to internalize where you want to go and to literally offer yourself support, a sort of mantra. Use the statements to build yourself up. It may seem silly at first, but do it anyway. After a while you will want to have a kind and supportive dialogue with yourself because you are internalizing your goals and what you have to offer. Being kind to yourself with your internal dialogue is, in my opinion, the most important thing you can do to treat yourself well and to put you on the right path to being your best self.

Speaking positively to yourself about all aspects of your life will be the beginning of a waterfall of positive happenings in your life. You may have heard about the book *The Secret* by Rhonda Byrne. It's a great and inspiring book as it focuses on the fact that you can't just say positive things and be done. Speak to yourself to believe, to become part of your subconscious mind. Then, turn those thoughts into action and those actions will manifest themselves as results. I'm not saying there is a free pass here. You have to do the work. If you speak positively to yourself and believe, then the work becomes part of an exciting and inspiring journey. In fact, it's really not work at all!

The Total Package

Now you're being kind to yourself, right? Fantastic! Now you need to look after the physical you. If you only look after getting your mind right and not your body, then you aren't really looking after the entire you. This encompasses many disciplines. You need to ask yourself if you have an outlet for stress. We all have some sort of stress in our lives and if you're not coping with it in a healthy manner, then trust me, it is doing damage to your person and maybe even to your interpersonal relationships.

I recommend some sort of exercise regime on a regular basis. This could be anything. I mentioned earlier that I have a Bowflex machine in my basement and an exercise bike. I find it difficult to get to the gym and I really do enjoy resistance training. This is my outlet to deal with stress and to take better care of myself. I also enjoy playing tennis. I like to exercise four to five times a week if I can for a half hour to forty-five minutes. Maybe you are a runner. That's great. Perhaps you prefer to do team sports. That's terrific! Do it. We're all different and have our own likes and dislikes. Maybe you don't exercise at all. I would recommend that you start. Heck, something as simple as walking your dog is all it takes. Even if you just go for a half hour walk three times a week you will see benefit.

Exercising gives you time to think and provides an outlet to get out whatever is bothering you. Some terrific side effects are that you may live longer. You will certainly be healthier, and in my case, it sets a great example for my children. Some people say that they don't have time to work out. I get it. I prefer to work out mid-morning, but was missing too many workouts because I have a lot of responsibilities to my career and my family so I had to make time. I started getting up an extra hour early. I don't like getting up extra early, but now I miss exercising too much if I don't get up and do it. It's quiet and I workout without any interruptions. I also get way more done in the morning because I'm energized. I also end up going to bed a little bit earlier too and don't miss out on my eight hours of sleep.

Diet is a big one too. I *love* to eat, especially things like cheese, pizza, hamburgers, and pasta. I know that eating such things on an ongoing basis may shorten my life span in the long run. It also makes me sluggish because I have trouble holding back on such foods. It's all right to eat these things once in a while, but since I'm exercising so why not get all the benefits of bettering my physical person.

If you're not sure how to start incorporating healthy eating into your love of food, here are a few things that have worked well for me. I like to work out and then have a protein smoothie in the morning for breakfast. I also watch my portion sizes during other meals and try to have the restraint not to overeat. My wife and I have a juicer and try to have a juice daily using vegetables and fruits. I'm not the biggest fan of eating veggies as is, so juicing allows me a great alternative, making sure I get the nutrients I need. I also try not to eat anything after six or seven in the evening. When we go out to eat at a restaurant I may order one of my favourite meals and enjoy all of it and that's okay. I deserve it because I don't do it very often and I don't beat myself up about it. It becomes a treat. The good news is that when you exercise, improving your diet becomes easier. You see, you're getting momentum going to improve yourself and I know it might be hard to imagine right now, but you're going to want to eat better and improve in other ways too. Not only that, but your body will naturally start to crave healthier foods to refuel after you exercise. It just becomes easier.

This brings me to another topic important for me and possibly for you. I used to drink alcohol with regularity and I now believe I was using it as a way to combat the stress of the day when I did a poor job at making time for exercise. I wasn't an alcoholic, but I would have one or two drinks later in the evening and relax on the couch.

I would stay up later because I was enjoying said beverage. I would also make poor eating decisions while I drank and would often snack during these times. This goes against my progress towards the battle of the bulge. Because I was up later, I would sleep later. I would miss out on finding time for exercise. So, I took control and stopped drinking completely. If you give something up, such as alcohol, and you miss it on an ongoing basis and find it difficult to continue on with its absence, then you may have a problem. This could be alcohol or it could be eating. I admit that I missed it for the first few nights, but soon after, I didn't miss it at all. Now I will still have an alcoholic beverage on a social occasion, but it is no longer a part of my regular life.

I wrote earlier about the importance of filling your mind with positive content whether from friends, television, radio, CD's, or literature. This is truly important to do on a daily basis, even if it is only for fifteen minutes. Personally, I fill my mind with positive, growth related learning daily, and grabbing the latest book I am reading or *Success Magazine* to read while I'm on the exercise bike. Other ways to do this include listening to audio books, or interviews with successful people, or with those making a difference or on subjects that focus on the personal journey of improvement. It doesn't even have to be long, a mere fifteen minutes of reading / listening before bed is all. There are plenty of ways to make time for that small interval of development. It's not so much in doing a whole lot at once, but more about consistency and filling your mind with the positive and keeping that tank of positive mindset full. It's like a chuck on the shoulder from a good friend on a daily basis letting you know you're all right and that you can do whatever you put your mind to doing.

Some other things that I find important to do are spending time with my wife and children. They mean the world to me and I love my time with them. At least weekly and sometimes a few times a week, my son and I will go to the zoo, the science center, or the local historical park with the train he loves to ride. It's just the two of us and it is important bonding time. I time block these hours into my week and do my best to protect this time I find so important. I want to be a present and attentive father. My wife and I also try to spend at least an hour or two together at the end of each day before bed. Sometimes we don't say a whole lot and we don't need to say anything. It's time with my best friend. We also try to book a date night once every two weeks in order to get out and have supper and connect just the two of us. I really look forward to these occasions. I also like to book at least two good vacations away with my family every year for a week to ten days at a time. It's just us reconnecting together without any distractions and for me; it's almost like heaven. These are the people who fill me up. Spend time with those who make you feel good and lift you up.

All of the above is about consistent quality, not quantity. Make these practices sustainable. These are things that, when done on a regular basis, feed me as a person and help me to feel in harmony with the world and myself. Yes, the stresses of everyday occur, but because of these things that I put into practice, I'm better equipped to deal with the issues and stressors that come up.

Your Best Investment

You need to invest in yourself. This means taking care of, and improving, yourself. It may mean spending money on you and not your family. Again, this is okay. Remember, sometimes it is all right to be selfish, and if it is for the benefit of you as a person, and the positives outweigh the negatives, then I strongly recommend you do it.

My wife wasn't thrilled when I purchased a huge, expensive Bowflex machine, but I knew I would use it and it would benefit me, so it was a worthwhile investment in myself. I like to purchase books and magazines where I find mentorship in my life. It comes at a cost, but again, I consider it an investment in me. I chose to spend the money on having a business coach. Many people wouldn't consider the expense worthwhile, but I considered it an investment in me and I have reaped the rewards.

These are things that I do for me and I highly recommend all of them. However, you are a unique human being and you have many talents, many of which may be untapped. You may not realize that you have them, but by doing things for you and investing in yourself you may find it a very worthwhile endeavour. Because I look after me and invest in me, I am in harmony with myself and open to exploring and exploiting my talents and the gifts I have to offer to the world. The good news is that you can do the very same. What is the next investment in you that you are going to make?

Opportunity Knocks

Call it karma. Call it the universe listening to you or infinite intelligence. Call it God listening and blessing you. If you get yourself in good harmony and open yourself up to opportunity and exploration in your life, then good things will begin to happen to you. I don't mean to sound like the message in a fortune cookie, but feeling good about yourself means you are ready to contribute in the way you were meant to contribute to the world.

Remember, I said you couldn't truly help others until you helped yourself. This is exactly what I was talking about. By doing all of the above you can't help but transform yourself into a more positive and healthy individual in all ways. When you are happy and replace the negative with the positive, then you begin to attract the positive. You may have heard some people complain that nothing good ever happens to them and they are negative and downtrodden. They are attracting what they are putting out to the world. It's a sad, but true realization. Imagine what kind of a world we would be living in if all of us were in a positive harmony with ourselves and what we, as a society, could accomplish. All of us have the ability to be better, to move toward a state of true happiness and create a better self and environment for you, your family, and your friends.

One of the most influential books of the 20th and 21st centuries is Napolean Hill's *Think and Grow Rich*. In developing this book, Hill interviewed successful people to discover what made the difference of being successful versus not. He wanted to know what kind of cloth these individuals were cut from to find great success. Friends, the answer to that question is the title of the book itself. I've given you the tools above to prepare you to think and grow. Everything starts with a thought. You can think and grow to whatever you want. You can aim to be rich. You can aim to be happy. You can aim to be both. You can aim to do whatever you want to do, but it begins by putting you in a good mental state. Now, are you ready to think and grow?

> "Friendship with one's self is all important, because without it one cannot be friends with anyone else in the world."
>
> - Eleanor Roosevelt

> "People often say that motivation doesn't last. Well, neither does bathing – that's why we recommend it daily."
>
> - Zig Ziglar

> "Great things are not done by impulse, but by a series of small things brought together."
>
> - Vincent Van Gogh

Chapter 5: Points for Self-Evaluation

- **Realize that you are the most important person in your life.**
- **Be kind to yourself in your internal dialogue.**
- **Dwell on the positive.**
- **Look after the whole you, mind and body.**
- **Recognize negative influences and eliminate them from your life.**
- **Add positives to your life.**
- **Invest in you!**
- **Think and grow to a better you.**

Chapter 6

Shift

"Change the way you look at things and the things you look at change."

- Wayne W. Dyer

The Chicken or the Egg?

How do you see the world around you? Do you go through your day angry, blaming others, and thinking that people that hurt you are evil beings? Many of us do. People get in our way. We can't control them. How about situations and circumstances? If you are stuck right now, it is likely because you only see one view of your situation or circumstance. We can't control the world around us, but we can control how we perceive the world around us and this opens up so many options and can allow you to change your circumstances and your worldview.

Which came first, the chicken or the egg? For many people they ponder this same question, but in relation to success and happiness. Many people wonder which comes first, happiness or success. The majority of people think that you must first find success to then find happiness. This is a flawed view of this conundrum. Success does not create happiness. This is evidenced by the countless stories we have all heard of people with money, with several homes throughout the world, and a perceived privileged lifestyle who say they are dissatisfied and unhappy. They feel something is missing. We all know somebody like this, believing that it is the situation that translates to happiness. Maybe it is a negative co-worker that lashes out at others. Maybe it is the teller at the bank who is constantly sour and rude, and you hope you won't get her or him when it is your turn in line. Is this person truly happy? Likely not. These people present themselves as on guard and defensive. They are like prickly porcupines to those around them. They are not happy and see the world as a bad place. Everybody is out to get them. The people around them are incompetent and are not to be trusted. This demeanour can happen to anybody, rich or poor. Such a negative view of the world breeds negativity into one's own life.

Yes, it is possible to have success without true happiness, but it won't last. Nothing is permanent on the outside, but true happiness, what is on the inside, can last. Make your life value-based; a life focused on what makes you happy and you can achieve long lasting results for success as you define it.

Shift

How do you start to find a place of happiness and, ultimately, peace so you can find your successes, whatever they may be? One thing you need to do is to change your perceived view of the world. You need to shift your viewpoint. It's easy to look at the nasty bank teller and think he or she is a terrible person. In fact, it's easy to think that anybody that is wronging you is terrible. Don't join these people in their negativity as they spew it. Change the way you look at such people. Look at that bank teller and realize that their actions are an indication of how he or she is hurting. Now their demeanour isn't so powerful or prickly to you. That person is in some kind of pain and that is why they are acting in such a way. All of us are ultimately good people at our core. Somewhere along the way many of us get lost and allow our assumptions about what we are supposed to do in life influence how we behave and live our lives. Clearly, I've done it. Don't take the easy worldview because it is that of the majority. Don't mirror society. Look deeper and you realize what is at the core of these individuals. Change your perception and you change your view of these people.

I don't know what your life looks like right now, but if you are reading this book then you are (hopefully) searching for more. You have a hunger to absorb as much knowledge as possible to be the best you that you can be. It's possible that you are not happy with your current circumstances, yet you continue along with the status quo because it is all you know and all you can see, but it doesn't make you happy. Consider looking at your situation from a different viewpoint. There is likely more than one way or view point to look at your circumstances and the world around you. Change your perception. With practice, options that you did not know existed will begin to appear to you.

Perceive Possibilities

In my own life I have realized that having the best intentions and thinking positive thoughts have not brought all the peace and happiness into my life that I had hoped would happen. John Maxwell says, "We cannot become what we need by remaining what we are." We have to change. We have to do all of the inner work and hone our skills to be able to rise above the norms set by society. This includes your worldview and being able to perceive situations differently, differently from the complacent perceptions society considers relevant. This means you need to be able to think outside of the box. You need to be able to perceive possibilities where others might not dare to venture. This may not be easy at first, but with practice it will become commonplace to you.

Some people are able to achieve what appears to be the impossible. How? Besides all of the planning and preparation, they first are able to perceive an outcome that others are not able to see. If everybody could see it and achieve it, the accomplishment would not be so incredible. A well-known example would be Sir Richard Branson. He has achieved in so many realms. From his business pursuits with Virgin Records, to the luxury airliner, Virgin Airlines; from being a successful author to attempting, and holding, world records. Richard Branson doesn't stop innovating. He is able to achieve because he sees such achievements as a reality where others simply do not. I would be willing to bet that his mindset is not, "Can I achieve it?" but rather, "How can I achieve it?" There's a big difference. One question involves some doubt, while the other is looking for the answer.

Not as incredible, but incredible to me, would be my changing my skewed viewpoint or perception of who I am and what I could achieve based on what I felt society expected of me. I took myself from a place of unhappiness to a place of happiness. Yes, I did all of the inner work to heal myself and to be a better me, but in order to achieve I also had to change my perception. I had to rise above and see all of the opportunity available for me and I would take the steps to reach for it. These are the same opportunities available to everybody, but remain hidden to the vast majority because of the inability to realize that you don't have to stick to the societal norms that were falsely set for you from your past experiences. I had to see that I could take a one hundred and eighty degree turn and achieve and thrive by doing what makes me happy. I had to be able to perceive this reality first, regardless of what I had previously thought society expected of me and what I thought I was pigeonholed to do. I was able to perceive another viewpoint. I didn't ask if I could do it, but rather how I could do it! I also had to recognize that my perception of myself was the only one that mattered because it was the only one I could actually change. Remember this, your perception is the only one that counts when it comes to your own success, whatever success looks like for you!

To achieve your true happiness and realize successes, you need to have the ability to stand above the crowd and all of the societal noise in order to gain a better view and perceive all of the options available to you. Don't fall into the trap of taking the easy societal way of perceiving people and situations. Being your best self means doing the work and rising above. Being able to see people and situations for what they truly are and then being able to perceive other actualities, will give you advantages and options that you never dreamed existed. If you can change your perception, you can change your world!

"If the doors of perception were cleansed, everything would appear to man as it is, Infinite. For man has closed himself up, till he sees all things thro' narrow chinks of his cavern."

- William Blake, The Marriage of Heaven and Hell

"No man has the right to dictate what other men should perceive, create or produce, but all should be encouraged to reveal themselves, their perceptions and emotions, and to build confidence in the creative spirit."

- Ansel Adams

"To change ourselves effectively, we first had to change our perceptions."

- Stephen R. Covey, The 7 Habits of Highly Effective People: Powerful Lessons in Personal Change

"How would your life be different if...you stopped making negative judgmental assumptions about people you encounter? Let today be the day...you look for the good in everyone you meet and respect their journey."

- Steve Maraboli, Life, the Truth, and Being Free

Chapter 6: Points for Self-Evaluation

- **Success does not create happiness. Happiness creates success.**
- **Don't take the easy societal way of perceiving people and situations.**
- **Shift your viewpoint; change your perceptions of other people.**
- **Perceive a reality where others cannot in order to achieve.**

Chapter 7

Thrive with Gratitude

"In the beginning there was nothing.
God said, 'Let there be light!' And there was light.
There was still nothing, but you could see it a whole lot better."

- Ellen DeGeneres

Why Gratitude?

While the title of this chapter may seem self-explanatory, it encompasses so many things within our lives. Don't shrug off this topic thinking you know it all. Examine all the things in your life in which you need to express your gratitude. No matter how bad you may think things are in your life, there are always many positives, things in which you can be grateful. Often times we don't pay enough attention to all of the good around us. We focus too much on the things we shouldn't be concentrating upon. We forget to be thankful! It comes down to not being able to see the forest for the trees. Fully understanding this chapter will better help you to excel in all aspects of your life.

By showing gratitude and by being thankful, you better put into perspective your own life. Remember that your thoughts affect your actions that further influence your course in life. It will also accelerate your growth and goal attainment. By making this exercise a part of your life, you better appreciate where you are, where you've come from and where you're going on your life's journey. The side effect is that others can also benefit from your gratitude and thankfulness. Later in this chapter I will speak to how I use gratitude daily in my own life for positive benefits, so that you too may make it an important exercise to do in your life.

Be Thankful

Examine your own life. What do you have? Do you have a roof over your head? Maybe it's not the home you want. Maybe you want to do some renovations. Put all of that aside. You are in your home for a reason. You must have liked something about it that you may now be forgetting. Think how fortunate you are to have a home! So many people would love to be in your position. Be thankful for your home.

Be thankful for your family and friends. Perhaps you have a significant other, or children, or some terrific friends. You are very fortunate to have some meaningful relationships in your life. To have another's love is priceless. Be thankful for your positive relationships. Celebrate them and don't be afraid to tell these same people how much you appreciate them. Without relationships, it would be difficult for us to exist and to excel. Relationships are a big part of why we are here on earth. Without relationships we wouldn't have any reason to contribute to society as a whole.

Be thankful for your occupation - even if it isn't your dream career yet. It helps to pay the bills and, in turn, helps you to survive. Many people need jobs. You are in an enviable position. Be thankful for your coworkers and for your clients, those that require your services. Having a job allows you to contribute to society. It does not matter what kind of a job you currently hold. Your contribution adds to the larger picture of society.

Be thankful for other people's triumphs. There is no other positive emotion to convey towards another than being happy when they succeed. Enjoy the moment with other people and celebrate them and their accomplishments. Don't allow jealousy into your mind. The new you is about being positive. In the long run, you too will benefit from this positive energy in which you are putting forth. Not only does it make the person who succeeded feel good and feel validated through your happiness for them, but you also will reap the rewards because of your happiness for them.

You are getting the idea about what I am talking about when I say to be "thankful." Look at the big picture. Look back ten or twenty years and see where you have come from. I know it may be easy to feel that life is stagnant or that you haven't accomplished anything, but this type of larger examination allows you to see where you have come from and how fortunate you truly are in your life. This doesn't mean that you can't strive for greater things, but maybe things aren't so bad. It feels good to know that good exists for yourself.

Give Thanks for Your Future Today

Be thankful for all of the things that you know you are going to achieve in the future. I know this may sound odd, but part of success is recognizing that you will achieve your goals. Believe it with all of your heart. What your conscious mind accepts as true will absolutely come to fruition. Give thanks for all of it right now!

Consider your personal and health goals. Be thankful for the end result right now! Consider your goals with your family. Give thanks for what you want to achieve in terms of family today! Consider your income goals. Perhaps you are starting a business and want a goal of making a million dollars annually in a few years. Give thanks for it right now!

I am thankful for all of the income streams that come to me which allow me to support my family. I am thankful for the gift of being able to make a difference in the lives of others. I am thankful that I have so much time that I spend with my family and that I can go on several vacations away with them. I am thankful that I am healthy and vibrant. How about you?

The Power of Thank You

How do you feel when you hear thank you for something that you've done? Good? Appreciated? Like you would want to help again? Thank you has the power to change an entire relationship.

If somebody does something for you, be gracious. Say thank you. Send thank you cards. Writing a quick note of thanks is something that really is a quick and easy process, yet the recipient will appreciate your efforts. Being gracious and thankful is a positive exercise for you personally, but you are also putting out positive energy into the world.

The words "thank you" may seem insignificant as written on this page, but when you say these words to another human being, it can be very powerful. To hear the sincere words of "thank you" from another can be extremely validating. It means your actions, whatever it was, helped another. It means I appreciate you. It means you are worthy. I'm sure all of us know people in our lives that say these words with the utmost sincerity. When they say thank you, does it not just make you want to respect them just a little bit more than you did before? These two words are much more than mere words on a page. They are relationship building words. They go towards building the integrity of the person saying thank you and they build up the person receiving the thanks.

When you travel to another country and you don't speak the language, I recommend that you learn to say "thank you" in the native tongue of the people of that country. No matter what the socio-economic standing of the other person, when you say "thank you," it is almost always welcomed. It brings a smile to the other person and if they are a hardened person, they soften when the words are conveyed with sincerity. It makes them want to be of assistance to you. Again, the words "thank you" are powerful, relationship building words.

Boomerang

As you put all the pieces together that we have discussed so far, you will find that expressing gratitude and being thankful becomes easier. It truly comes down to getting back what you put out into the world. I'm not saying you should expect praises from people for being gracious. You should always give with the expectation of receiving nothing in return. The good news is that the universe just doesn't work that way. It's like a boomerang. It comes back to you. This goes hand in hand with what I was saying about focusing on the positive. To live a truly rich life, don't just focus on achievement, focus on fulfillment. Gratitude helps you with being fulfilled.

One quick side note: Early on in my own personal development, I thought I was being very positive. However, in hindsight, I think I was being cocky and a little arrogant. It really only got me so far. My attitude and approach were flawed. I started out as I am going to accomplish X and I'm going to make X amount of money. I'm a good person and I deserve it. This isn't the guy that I really wanted to be either. There is nothing wrong with being confident as all of the exercises will make you more confident, but there is a difference between being confident and being arrogant.

By doing further research and reading I started to put together all of the previous topics of discussion and added gratitude. When you are truly thankful and show gratitude, love radiates from within you. It may not at first. It takes time to practice and to fully grasp the reasons for gratitude. It's just plain being thankful and acknowledging it on a daily basis. When I take a few moments to myself and concentrate on all the reasons I have to be thankful in this world, I am almost moved to tears and I am so humbled. It changes something within me. I become a little softer and less rugged. I am more approachable and loving. I am more open and accessible. This doesn't just mean open and accessible to people, but also to the positive opportunities that await me. I am more accepting and appreciative of my destiny as it unfolds itself to me.

Practice Gratitude

I personally practice the act of gratitude daily. I may wake up and not feel very grateful initially, but I sit down and focus on all the goodness in my life. I put these things that I am grateful for into words and allow myself to feel the emotion about all the goodness around me and in my life. I do it in the morning before I sit at my desk or go to appointments, usually while enjoying a cup of coffee. I use a gratitude journal. Depending on what is going on, I may have more than one going at a given time. Currently I have two.

In the first, I record the date and write a few sentences of appreciation and gratitude revolving around my wife. It could be something that she did or how she interacts with me or our children or somebody else. It could be about how she makes me feel or the sacrifices that I notice she makes for our children and myself. The point is that I write daily about how I appreciate my wife. It is easy to take one's marital partner for granted. Being a parent can sometimes put a marital relationship in second place as you work together to keep the house together and look after your children. My journal involving my wife keeps me focused on our relationship. I simply love her too much to ever take her for granted.

In the second journal, I record the date and start with the words, "Today I am thankful for..." Then I record three things for which I am thankful. It could be from that morning or the previous day. It could be a simple observation of something that I might normally take for granted. I notice that, when I look back in my journal, there is a theme of appreciation around family. I appreciate my children. I appreciate my wife. I also appreciate little things, like a phone call from somebody I haven't spoken to in awhile. I appreciate small opportunities in my business that allows me to assist somebody else and put food on our family table.

Keeping a journal is not complicated. When I started it was a fairly cursorily exercise. Then my emotions started to take over after just a few entries. It reminds me of what is important in my life and it puts me in the right mindset to assist others and achieve happily. It makes me a better father, husband, and businessman. It is a very grounding, humbling, and Zen-like exercise. I find that it is the perfect way to start each day. At the end of the day, I try to again be thankful and reflect in my own mind upon the good that occurred that day or about what I learned. I do this as I lay on my pillow before drifting off to sleep. Put simply, gratitude bookends my day.

All of us experience adversity. I have found that gratitude has helped me to better handle difficult or challenging experiences. Sometimes it takes a few minutes to wrap my head around the issue, but I think it through and remember all of the positives in my life and I am much less deterred. Did anybody die? Did anybody get seriously injured? If the answer to these two questions is no, then it isn't so bad. I can handle it. In the big picture of life it is a speed bump. To be honest, I think this has surprised my wife. In the past I may have lost my temper and been very upset with certain challenges that have come to us. I rarely do that anymore. Again, I weigh the experience against the big picture and it often pales in comparison. There is no reason to get upset. Life's little happenings don't really have to be a huge crisis. They are what you make them.

And what if there is a catastrophic event in your life, like the loss of a loved one or a serious illness that befalls someone that is close to you? Of course bad things happen that are out of our control and I would never minimize any of these events, but by habitually practicing gratitude, you can somehow remain a little more grounded. Yes, it is upsetting, but remember that it is out of your control. It's all right to grieve or to be upset. This is a part of the natural process of such events. Just remember that you are not alone. Everybody has a story. Your job is to do your best to live your life well.

Gratitude also helps you to better appreciate your past. Appreciate where you have been. I have been able to do that in my own life and am so thankful to come from loving parents. In hindsight, I am glad to have endured the experiences I had because they have taught me so much. In fact, if I think back to all of my difficult experiences and then ask myself to what degree did I make it through those experiences, I would have to say I have made it through one hundred percent of the time. I'm still here and you're reading this book so you too have made it through one hundred percent of the time. You learn far more from sailing troubled seas than you do smooth waters. I'm thankful I have taken lessons from sailing my own troubled seas, and I better know how to avoid choppy water when it presents itself.

Without gratitude you cannot realize true harmony and success. Be humble and be truly thankful. This is integral to your personal growth and to being your best you. The words of the first verse of *Amazing Grace*, written by John Newton, are those of a spiritual song. It was a song that was chosen at my father's funeral. For some time afterwards, every time I heard this hymn I became choked up. As I became stronger, I examined the words and found comfort and meaning in my own life.

> *Amazing Grace! How sweet the sound*
> *that saved a wretch like me!*
> *I once was lost, but now am found;*
> *was blind, but now I see.*

For me the words are about how fortunate I truly am. I have so much to be thankful for in my life. For a while, I couldn't see all that was good around me, but now I can. My eyes are open and I am so very thankful. Amazing Grace!

"Cultivate the habit of being grateful for every good thing that comes to you,
and to give thanks continuously. And because all things have contributed
to your advancement, you should include all things in your gratitude."

- Ralph Waldo Emerson

"Acknowledging the good that you already have in your life is the foundation
for all abundance."

- Eckhart Tolle, A New Earth: Awakening to Your Life's Purpose

"When you are grateful, fear disappears and abundance appears."

- Anthony Robbins

"Be thankful for what you have; you'll end up having more. If you concentrate on what you don't have, you will never, ever have enough."

- Oprah Winfrey

Chapter 7: Points for Self-Examination

- Be thankful for everything in your life.
- Be thankful for the goals you will achieve.
- Be thankful and accelerate your personal growth and goal attainment.
- The words, "thank you," are powerful, relationship building words.
- Being thankful is rewarding to you.
- Make time daily to practice gratitude.

Chapter 8

Your Untapped Power Within

"The possibilities of creative effort connected with the subconscious mind are stupendous and imponderable. They inspire one with awe."

- Napoleon Hill

The Missing Link Rationalized

To me, the power of the subconscious mind is incredibly intriguing and exciting. It is absolutely amazing what the mind can accomplish. I am not an expert in this topic, but I am a student of this phenomenon. As a student, I have applied these same principles in my life with great success.

Studies have shown that we utilize very little of our brains. Why is that? I can't even fathom what is missing from our brain functioning, but if we utilize so little and think we are using all of the capacity we require for life, then imagine how incredible things could be if we figured out how to use more.

I truly believe that this is the missing link as to why some individuals are so happy and successful and why others are not. The exciting part is that all of us have the capacity to achieve both happiness and success. Before we delve in any further, let's examine what many people consider to be coincidences.

Sometimes things occur that seem somewhat unexplainable. Have you ever had the experience of thinking of somebody, for whatever reason, and then your telephone rings and it is that person calling you. Perhaps they call you and you say, "I was just thinking about you and felt I had to call." Maybe you rarely talk to this person, yet they reached out to you. Why is that? Is it mere coincidence? Did you will it to happen?

Have you ever been on vacation to somewhere far away and you run into some friends that you have not seen in a long while? Out of seven continents, and all of the countries in the world, and you run into people you know. Isn't that pretty incredible? Is it coincidence?

The following has happened to me. I had been having such a terrific experience with my current car. After having had cars that have had various issues and breakdowns, I felt fortunate to have found such a good car. I was thinking, and quite out of the blue, "It must be time for my car to break down. It's due because all of my cars seem to break down." Within a couple of days, my car broke down and I needed a tow. Is that coincidence? Maybe.

Many such occurrences that happen to us are dismissed as coincidence. The definition of coincidence as found in the Oxford Dictionary is: "A remarkable concurrence of events or circumstances without apparent causal connection." I believe that to dismiss such chance happenings as a mere coincidence is to truly take away from the intelligence that we, as human beings, possess, simply because we cannot explain it. That's one thing humans do well. We rationalize things, especially those things we cannot explain.

Perhaps you have been struggling with a problem that has been challenging you for some time. For the life of you, you cannot seem to find an answer. Then all of a sudden it just comes to you. Perhaps you awoke from sleep and had to write down some notes immediately for fear that you might not remember the answer in the morning. Why is it that answers can sometimes just suddenly show up? Is it possible that your subconscious mind had been silently looking for the solution, putting it out to the world and then the answer appeared? Yes! It is possible. In fact, many great inventors and theorists have received the answer that solves their invention or theory, the missing link if you will, in times of quiet when they weren't even consciously thinking about the challenge. Isn't that truly incredible? The mind is so powerful that it works even when we think it is not.

Have you been sitting, chatting with friends when you stop because you are having a déjà vu moment? Perhaps you were traveling in a country you had never visited before when you feel you had already lived that particular moment in time. There are all sorts of medical theories as to why déjà vu occurs, although there is nothing absolutely concrete. Psychotherapists and psychologists have their theories and parapsychologists have their own ideas, but there is no particular theory that reigns resolute for why déjà vu occurs. This is another occurrence that many people have experienced that seems unexplainable. Perhaps there is more going on than can be rationalized. Perhaps our minds, our brains, are more powerful than we know or can truly understand.

If you really think about it, aren't all of the above incidences truly incredible? Why do these things happen? Why do we simply dismiss these things instead of trying to learn how to harness and understand the circumstances that surround these occurrences? Do these things just happen, or do we have the power within us to make such things happen? I believe the power lies within each and every one of us.

An Illustration of Belief

Whether you believe in God, that the universe listening to you, or in positive energy, it does not matter. What I'm going to tell you about absolutely works. What you put out there, what you concentrate upon fully and completely will come to fruition. Understand that this may not be immediate, but if you keep your focus long enough, you will achieve what you want to achieve. The example in the next paragraph is truly remarkable.

When I was thirteen years old, my Mom was diagnosed with a brain tumour the size of a grapefruit. She was given three weeks to live. The plan was to do surgery, but we were told that if she survived, she would likely never walk or talk again. I was never so scared in my whole life. Our entire family was in shock. During the time before the surgery, my Mom would often try to sit me down and discuss what was likely going to be the inevitable, given the odds. She tried to tell me that my Dad would likely want to remarry a few years down the road and that I should accept his new wife as my mother. I wasn't having any of it. I told her that she was going to be all right. I had been praying. You may remember me saying that I came from a very devout Protestant family. In the Bible, it says to pray and believe that what you are asking has already been done and it will be so. This is exactly what I was doing. With the innocence and full belief of a child, I prayed with conviction and with the full belief that God would get my Mom through the surgery. In my mind there was no alternative; what I was asking for and wanting would absolutely occur.

After the surgery, the surgeon asked my father if he was a religious man. My Dad said that he was religious. The surgeon said that it was a miracle. The tumour had miraculously shrunk without any medical intervention prior to the surgery to about one inch in diameter. My mother could talk, although a little slurred when tired (but who of us doesn't). She went from a bed to a wheelchair, to a walker, to a cane, to walking unassisted. In my mind, God had answered my prayer.

I think many of us have heard such incredible stories. Are they miracles? Is it the true power of the subconscious mind at work? We may never know or truly understand. Currently, this is part of being human. We don't understand. It's also biblical that we lack the understanding as to why things occur; we lack the capacity to understand the higher power at work. I do believe that with practice, we can harness this misunderstood power.

Dogma of Belief

Whether or not you believe in God and the Bible, there are some incredible pieces of wisdom within the book itself. To pray and have faith is to believe fully. If you did not pray as I did, but still believed fully that everything would work out, then perhaps you were putting your belief and faith in an outcome, and were then releasing this positive energy to the universe, hence forming a positive outcome. Please know that to do this you must absolutely omit all of the negativity of thoughts to the contrary. I know that my Christian brethren may not accept my point of view, and I'm not saying my mother's immediate change in tumour size was not a miracle by God, but without God, could it be that my full belief in the outcome helped to create the outcome? I'm certain that my father, my siblings, our friends, and the congregation at church were praying for the best. It could be that the power of prayer healed my mother. It could also be that all of the positive energy that was being put forth into the universe also had an effect on the outcome with my Mom. Perhaps it was just the right amount of positivity and/or prayer. Perhaps any less would mean a different outcome?

Things happen to people. People endure terrible illnesses and pass away. I'm not saying that a loved one, or the afflicted person, did not pray with belief that they would be healed. Sometimes we cannot intervene when it comes to urgent health issues, but sometimes incredible things do happen. I think all of us have heard about an individual that was given a very small window of survival due to an illness, perhaps only a few months, but beat the odds and lived a few years longer. I would care to wager that the individual refused to accept the prophesized outcome. Again, sometimes things occur and we do not truly understand why. I still believe that we can intervene in certain circumstances because of the incredible power of the human mind.

Let's look at a different example. Let's again examine the story of comedian and A-list actor, Jim Carrey. There were times when, as a child, Jim and his family had to live out of a van on the streets of Toronto.[5] As a teenager, his father would drive him from gig to gig so that he could practice his comedic art and hopefully make it big.

---

[5] Jacques, Renee. 16 Wildly Successful People Who Overcame Huge Obstacles to Get There. *Huffington Post*. TheHuffingtonPost.com, Inc. Sept. 25, 2013. June 11, 2015. http://www.huffingtonpost.com/2013/09/25/successful-people-obstacles_n_3964459.html.

It would be easy for Jim to accept the current family circumstances as his future outcome, but he believed so deeply that he would make a huge impact and become a great actor that he wrote himself a cheque for $10,000,000![6] He carried that cheque around with him knowing that one day he would receive a cheque in that same amount. He believed that this outcome was not a matter of *if*, but rather a matter of *when* it would happen. Not only did he make it and attain his goal, but he has done it over and over again.

Something else that I like in the Bible is that it says that man was created in the image of God. To me this means that God has given us the potential to do amazing feats and I don't think we fully understand the potential available within us. There are many incredibly happy and successful non-believers in the world. This is not a coincidence! They practice having the full focus and belief in the outcomes they want to create. They write down their goals. They speak to what they are doing. Naysayers do not sway them, but rather, they have unwavering belief that they will be successful. They act as though the goal is a done deal. This is exactly what you need to do. You need to believe that it is so. Then, it is done!

As mentioned, there is great wisdom in the Bible that can be applied to personal accomplishment. This type of thinking is faith at work. Surely, there are other great nuggets of wisdom that come from other religious teachings in which can be applied to personal accomplishment, but what if you believe in the power of the universe, or you require a different explanation because you are not religious? This too requires faith.

Everything around us, including ourselves, is made of matter. When we think thoughts and put them out to the universe, we are engaging the matter around us. You could consider that the matter around us is carrying our message to the universe, whether positive

---

[6] Wikipedia, the free encyclopedia. Jim Carrey. *Wikipedia, The Free Encyclopedia*. Wikimedia Foundation, Inc. June 3, 2015. June 11, 2015. http://en.wikipedia.org/wiki/Jim_Carrey.

or negative. We already know that we receive what we dwell upon. With this in mind, the universe will bring to you what you put out to it.

Keep in mind that you can believe that God is working on your behalf or that the universe is working on your behalf. I am of Christian faith, but I'm not advocating that you choose either way. It really does not matter for which belief system or ideology you attribute success. The message is still the same. Believe with unwavering faith that it is done. What you are asking for will come to you as long as you focus upon it and believe whole-heartedly that it will come to you.

Good Vibrations

Human beings have the ability to create. We have the ability to create new materials. We can create new and exciting contraptions. We can create art and music. We can also create the life we want to live. All of the above takes effort. As with anything worth doing in life, there will be challenges on the journey to success. Notice what I just did in that last sentence. I didn't say there would be no problems or failures, but instead I used the word challenges. Happiness and success does not dwell on an issue. Any issue can be overcome. Look for the solution and move forward. It is temporary. Take action. Full belief and conviction in your goals will allow you to plow through the challenges. Again, you are putting your full belief out to the world, to the universe. I don't mean that you are screaming it from the mountaintops, but you are not shy about it either. You need to radiate your conviction as though you are vibrating inside. I have done this and I have felt it. It is exciting and to use the word vibrating seems to me to be the best description I can afford to you. I have found that putting forth this vibration out into the universe brings answers. It creates solutions to roadblocks when before it seemed that there were none.

Some believe, including myself, that the goal-orientated vibration you put out to the world is, in essence, positive and therefore, you attract more positive energy to open doors that might otherwise be shut on your journey to your goals. Likewise, putting negative energy attracts more negative energy. This is why so few people really get it. They dwell on the negative and when they try to be positive, well, they will often retire to what they are used to and what is comfortable and easy to them. They fall back into concentrating on the negative, so that is exactly what life delivers to them. It's easy to be negative. Man is wired as a caveman: to always be looking for the negative, looking for threats. It's a survival instinct, but we are so much more intelligent than that caveman, or cavewoman, than we used to be. The challenge is to change your wiring. It takes practice and diligence to focus on the positive, but doing so brings more good things into your life. I challenge you to rise above.

As I said, this absolutely works. Drill into your subconscious mind with as much positivity and belief as you can. Put it out to the universe with your unwavering belief that your goals are being achieved as you live and breathe. Start to take action and watch what happens. This is why the guy with the grade seven education is sometimes more happy and successful than the guy with the master's degree. It's all about mindset, faith, conviction, and action. It's available to all of us, you just need to tap into it.

Knowing that you have the power within you to achieve anything you want by tapping into your subconscious mind, do you still think that coincidences really happen? As human beings, we have so much potential that we don't fully understand. I believe all of us are like sleeping Jedi-knights. As Yoda would say, "do or do not. There is no try." It is this kind of thinking, this absolute black and white belief in your goals that bring them to fruition. Now, next time something happens to you that you think is a coincidence, think again.

"To strengthen the connection between your conscious mind and your subconscious mind is to gain access to a map and compass to help you move towards your dream. To gain access to the subconscious mind is to gain the ability to see and create the future, the ability to shift the present, and the ability to alter your own perceptions of the past."

- Kevin Michel, Moving Through Parallel Worlds To Achieve Your Dreams

"We've all experienced pondering a problem all day long only to find we receive the solution when forgetting about the problem and thinking of something else. When we stop concentrating so hard, we allow our subconscious to flourish, and those who do this more than others are often called geniuses."

- James Morcan, The Orphan Conspiracies: 29 Conspiracy Theories from The Orphan Trilogy

"Faith consists in believing what reason cannot."

- Voltaire, The Works: Voltaire

Chapter 8: Points for Self-Evaluation

- There are no coincidences.
- Full, unwavering belief in an outcome can bring about its occurrence.
- Faith is not just about religion.
- Radiate your conviction for your goals as though you are vibrating inside and believe in its attainment.
- You have the power within you to do anything by tapping into your subconscious mind.

Flourish

Chapter 9

The Compass

"To reach a port, we must sail—Sail, not tie at anchor—Sail, not drift."

- Franklin Roosevelt

Resolve to Make Change

As humans, we are generally creatures of habit. We continue to do the same things day in and day out. It's not enough to simply resolve to take action; you need to make change. Most people want things to remain the same, but to be better. This will not be the case. You must get out of your comfort zone and do something different. Albert Einstein said, "The definition of insanity is doing the same thing and expecting a different result." I love that quote and I have certainly lived it, in the past. I understand that change can be scary, but this isn't necessarily a bad thing. In fact, if you aren't a little bit scared, then you aren't taking giant enough steps to make change.

I have no doubt that all of you reading this has heard about goal setting. "You need to set goals and you need to write them down. If you don't put your goals on paper, then they are just thoughts in your head. If they are not written down then they are simply a dream." The reality, these statements are all true. Putting them on paper makes them more tangible and creates a reference for you to look at from time to time. Successful and fulfilled people take the time on a regular basis to plan and reflect. I too have found that this is important in my own life. This is part of goal setting.

Find Your "Why," Your True Values

You may remember that you need to know your "why" in your life. This is really just your true value system. What is most important to you in your own life? You want all of your goals to be congruent with your "why." This will allow you to know your purpose. It is a higher calling and is great motivation. If you can hold your values as the center point, the highest priority in your life, then you will be a much happier individual. You will know why you want to attain your goals.

If you are having difficulty answering the above question, then I encourage you to perform the next exercise. If you only had six months left to live and you would be completely healthy until your last few seconds on earth and knew that you would expire at said time, how would you spend the remainder of your life? Don't let money stand in your way. Answer this question as though money were not a non-factor.

For me personally, I would like to spend it with my immediate family. I would spend as much time as possible with my wife and children. I would likely travel and visit all of my brothers and sisters and their families. I would also go to see my good friends. With my family at my side, I would travel to places that bring me joy and tranquility, enjoying and savouring every moment with them. I would also spend time doing other things that I enjoy, such as my morning exercise routine. I would spend some time in quiet reflection with my thoughts. I would quietly read inspiring material. If available, I would like to leave something behind. Perhaps it would be a scholarship program for youth wanting to better their lives or perhaps it would be a sizeable charitable donation.

My values focus around my relationships with my wife and children. My values focus around family travel. My values focus around time for me with exercise and in reading and quiet contemplation. My values focus on trying to leave the world a little bit better than when I arrived in it. Most of all, I want to matter to my family. These things are my "why." What are yours?

Create Your Personal Mission Statement

Now that you have your "why" in life clarified, you want to make sure you keep it at the forefront of your mind. Your personal goals can be wide and far reaching, but you want to ensure that you have a clear picture of what is most important to you. If you lose sight of these values, then you have a much higher probability of losing what brings you the greatest joy in your life. I'm talking about your personal happiness.

My personal mission statement goes a little something like this:

To be a present and attentive husband and father, making quality time with my family a priority. To take a minimum of two extended family vacations abroad to relax, re-charge and find perspective, enjoying other cultures as a family each year. To take daily me time to exercise and to fill my mind with positive, self-enriching material. To respect other people, listen to them and see their perspective. To passionately work to serve and enrich the lives of others, while being a contributor to the greater good of the universe around me.

By keeping my mission statement close at all times, regardless of how voraciously I work towards my goals, I am better in tune with what is most important to me as a person and to my personal happiness. Remember, you need to be a better you first, before you can truly have personal happiness and success. I will reflect upon my personal mission statement as I pursue my goals. I am the most important person in the world to me. It is the very same for you.

What do You Want in Life?

Now that you know your "why," you need to decide what you want in life. This is a pre-cursor to goal setting. You can't set goals unless you know what you want to do with your time here on earth. Some people don't really know what they want in life. That's all right. The good news is that deep down you really do want something. You just need to give yourself permission to recognize, acknowledge, and have it.

If you are still having difficulty with answering this question, then I will offer the following exercise. Write your own obituary. Don't write it from the perspective of today, but write it from the perspective of ten, twenty, forty, sixty-five years down the road. How do you want to be remembered? What impact do you want to make while you are alive? Don't be shy with this exercise. I know it may seem a little macabre, but have fun with it.

Currently, I would like my obituary to read something like the following, and preferably not to be read in the papers for at least another forty-five years:

> Today, Patrick Murray passed away in his sleep at his home on the Maui coast. While initially sad for our family, we are so blessed to have had his love, compassion, and wisdom while here on earth. To his family he will always be remembered as a loving and doting husband, father, and grandfather, who would never allow any of us to accept any boundaries to our lives. We will never forget the many wonderful family vacations together. We will miss his generous hugs that made us feel so loved and protected. To many, he was so much more, but to us he was just Patrick; Dad; Grandpa.
>
> Born and raised in Moose Jaw, Saskatchewan in 1973, Patrick met the love of his life at SIAST Wascana Campus in Regina, while obtaining his diploma in Dental Hygiene. He and Colette moved to Calgary, Alberta in 2001 and married in 2004. Colette gave birth to a beautiful son, Declan and later to a stunning little girl, Lyric. They were the apple of Patrick's eye and brought Patrick so much joy.
>
> Patrick later engaged in a bustling real estate career spanning over 25 years. He brought on other agents to assist with the demand. Patrick was known for his honest and easy going style. He always did his best to help his

clients and stayed in touch with many of them until his passing.

One of Patrick's greatest accomplishments is the writing of several books on the subject of personal development and the business he ran and loved, assisting those that wanted to live the life they truly wanted and longed for and in assisting companies with corporate culture. Founding The Murray Institute for Growth, he has travelled extensively speaking on the above topics and has certified over 10,000 individuals on his teachings to be a better you. Patrick loved sitting one-on-one with clients who wanted to live rich lives focused on values, and he helped many to realize that they can have it all in their own lives. He remained active in the business to the very end.

Patrick had many other businesses, too many to mention here. We know that all that came in contact with him will miss him dearly. He was very proud of his initiatives he set up to assist youth with learning the principles of self-development. While never a graduate of the University of Saskatchewan, he was an avid contributor to education and loved books. He was deeply honoured when the library was renamed the Patrick Murray Library.

Patrick loved fast cars and travel. He will always be remembered as the "older gentleman driving the Ferrari." He exercised every day and had no difficulty keeping up with the grandchildren. He took two extensive vacations yearly without fail with his wife and often other family members would join them. He was always approachable and made people feel special. He always made people a priority. We will miss you, until we meet again.

As I said, have fun with it! From this exercise I hope you can find out at least a few things that you want to accomplish while here on earth. I want to be a present and attentive father, but I also aspire to assist others in any way that I can. I also want to be able to enjoy travel and a few material items, although not my focus. I want to be healthy until the end. It looks like I have some lofty goals. I have no idea how to attain many of them and that is just fine. That's part of the fun in life. You don't have to know the answers to have the goals; you just have to set the goals.

Try this exercise and see how you want to be remembered and what you want to accomplish. This is a great starting point for you to create some goals to bring about the desired results you want in your life.

Get a Compass

Now get ready to set some goals. Think of goals as your compass for where you want to go and what you want to achieve in your life. I would recommend that you look at where you want to be in five years, in three years, in one year and in one month. Make goals for each of these time frames. Where will you be and what do you plan to have accomplished? I recommend that you make headings for each goal period. My own plan outline for one year looks a little like this:

My 1-Year Goals

- Health

- Personal

- Family

- Work/Career

    • Sub-headers for different business interests

If you want to do something similar, here is how I recommend breaking down each goal heading.

Under the Health heading, make a list of health related goals, such as how many times per week you want to work out and what activities you will do, weight training, biking, or running. You can also make a goal of the weight you want to be at and the kind of meals you will be eating, including portion sizes and alcohol intake.

Under the Personal heading, write things down that you will do for yourself. This is where you put in such things as the allotted time you want to have to reflect, think, and plan and will include how often you intend to do this activity. Write down how often and for how long you will fill my mind with positive literature in which you can use for motivation and growth. Personally, I schedule a minimum of 15 minutes a day and try to do a half hour if I can.

Under the Family heading, record the time you want to spend alone with each member of your family. Be sure to include family activities, as well as family vacations under this heading.

The Work/Career heading is where you record your work related goals. Because I always have a few endeavours going at a given time, I make sub-headings for each business opportunity I may be working on. This helps to keep every goal sorted and not seem as lofty. Put in deadlines, important contacts you need to make, calls to be made, a dollar amount you want to achieve for each activity. You may even put in marketing goals if they apply.

Start with your five-year plan. If you know exactly how you are going to reach your goal(s) then you are not thinking big enough. In fact, maybe your career goals or family goals don't even reflect the career or family that you currently have. That's just fine. This is about what you truly want and where you feel your destiny lies. Then do your three-year plan and make a list of where you will be on your journey to accomplish those five-year goals. Next make your one-year plan and plot what you want to accomplish in order to move you toward your three-year goals.

Write About Success

When you make your five, three and one-year goals, write in point form what you want to achieve, but then do more. If you really want to have true success and achieve your goals, then I encourage you to write about them. Write about each goal for any given period. This will be much like journaling. Record what you want to achieve and why you want to achieve it. Write about what you expect to be doing come the deadline. Write about how it will make you feel. How will this goal affect you and your family? How will it affect your business? Write some thoughts down about the steps you will take to achieve each goal. This process helps to make your goals more tangible. Your subconscious will begin to internalize what you are going to accomplish. This may seem "artsy-fartsy" to some, but if you really want to succeed, then you need to do this important exercise. Whether you are a Type A or a Type B personality, there are no shortcuts.

Journaling about your five, three, and one-year goals may seem labour intensive. I'll tell you right now that, yes, it is in fact, a little labour intensive. Some people run from opportunity because it comes in work clothes. Understand right now that opportunity always has work attached to it. Consider this the first portion of work to be able to reach your goals. The good news is that this is work that is all about you and your goals. It is the most worthwhile activity you can do. I like to take a full day, and sometimes even two or three days, to plan and write about my goals in depth. You may think this is excessive and that you can't make this happen. I used to be the same way until I truly understood how important this was to internalizing what I was going to accomplish in my subconscious mind. I take a few days between Christmas and New Years to write about my goals. I look forward to it, because it is a time of reflection on what I have already accomplished and the exciting adventure I am planning for me!

Brian Tracy highlights a longitudinal study following graduating high school students on his CD set, *The Psychology of Achievement*. These students were encouraged to write down their goals on an ongoing basis. After twenty years, only three percent of the students actually started and stayed with the practice. That same three percent was collectively worth more financially than the whole of the other ninety seven percent of the students that did no planning. Friend, if that doesn't make you want to do this practice then I don't know what will. Think about how great your family life would be if you were to plan for the betterment of your relationships with them. And remember, goals don't just need to apply to financial gain. You can live a wealthy life in so many ways. Wealth is yours to define.

Plan Each Leg of the Journey

If you are going on a long trip, you will certainly want to know where you want to end up, but is impossible to get there all at once. You need to plan each leg of your long journey. When it comes to reaching your goals, you need to break your goals down into smaller incremental goals and tasks.

Make goals for the current month. Using the same headings for your one-year goals (Health, Personal, Family, Work / Career), write what you want to accomplish that month that will begin you on the journey to reach your larger goals. These monthly goals become your action plan. Go a little beyond what you think you can achieve and try your best to make it so. You will re-make a monthly goal set for each month. I spend some quiet time at the end of every month planning my next month. You can keep these goals in point form, as I do, or write about them in-depth as you did with your five, three, and one-year goals. Refer to your one-year goals to make sure you are staying on track to achieving what you set forth to achieve.

To help you move towards your monthly goals, make a weekly goal list on Sunday afternoon or evening for the upcoming week. This can just be a point form list. Refer to your monthly goal list to make sure you are working towards accomplishing that month's goals. Keep it visible all week. I also like to sit down at the end of each day for a few minutes and make a list of goals or action plans that I want to achieve for the next day. I refer to my weekly list and each day I put down one or two items from that list in which I want to get accomplished along with all of the other tasks I want to get done that day. Keep this list visible along with that of your weekly goal list for constant reference.

I know that when you see all the things you need to get completed in a day that it can sometimes be a little daunting. Utilize a little bit of psychology on yourself. List a few things that you have already completed that day, but did not include on your list. This might include working out or fifteen minutes of personal development reading. By doing this, you give yourself a head start of sorts. You will see as you start your day that you have already checked off a few of the tasks for the day, giving you a head start on accomplishing all of your daily tasks. Likewise, if you happen to add and achieve a task, write it down too, and check it off your list. By seeing that you are accomplishing tasks on your list you can immediately see progress on your list and will feel invigorated and less overwhelmed at the start of your day.

Success Tips

Every day I look at the goals I have set for the week and goals I have set for that day. At the end of each week I refer to my monthly goal list. At the end of each month I refer to my yearly goal list. At the end of each year I refer to my three-year and five-year goal list. Don't beat yourself up if you don't accomplish what you set out to in a particular week or month. By setting lofty goals, you are not trying to set yourself up for failure, but rather you are going out of your comfort zone. Remember that you treat yourself more gently now and you fill your mind with positive self-talk, even when you don't reach all of your goals. If you aim for the stars, you will at least hit the moon, and if you do hit the stars you will feel truly accomplished. By doing this and taking the steps to reach your goals, you will be truly amazed at what you will have accomplished at the end of a year.

Because you have been working on yourself and have been seeking out your core values, make sure your action plans are consistent with your values. This ensures you are working harmoniously with yourself and will, in turn, help to ensure your happiness. I know that you will want to achieve all of your goals immediately. Don't be deterred. Remember that there is no such thing as instant gratification, but the consistent, small improvements you make on a daily basis will lead to huge results. What stands between you and your goal is your behaviour. That means that your actions must be in congruence with what you want to achieve. If your actions are congruent, then success is what you will attract by the person you become.

Make sure your goals are focused on the positive. As an example, if you have a lot of debt you want to pay off, don't make the focus of your goal to pay off debt; otherwise you may focus on debt. You get what you focus on. Make the focus of your goal around making money. If you are making money, the debt will take care of itself. Just be sure that your goals focus on positive outcomes and you will reap the appropriate rewards.

When you are goal setting, also think about the things that are sabotaging your success. What is holding you back from attaining your goals? Do your best to eliminate or reduce the said activity that is holding you back from achievement. Are they in alignment with your values? The more you can make sure that your daily activities are focused around meeting your goals, the better chance you have at achieving your goals. A little trick to do this is imagining being out of your body observing yourself doing daily activities. What practices could you eliminate that are not prudent to reaching your goals and what could you be doing instead? As yourself, what can you do today that will get you closer to reaching your goals? There is always something you can be doing to further your efforts.

Take time at the end of each month to look back and review what you have accomplished. By looking back and observing your progress made instead of just looking ahead to what you want to inevitably accomplish, you buoy your confidence and feel better about your progress and the attainment of your goals. Again, this is a little bit of personal psychology, but it works. Think about going on a long cross-country road trip from point A to point B. The driving time and all of the stops and sightseeing may take you weeks or even months. Initially it can be daunting looking at the long journey ahead, but when you look at how far you have come, especially later on in your trip when you are getting fatigued and just want to get there, it makes that last bit seem much less insurmountable. In fact, you may find new energy or a new reserve, if you will, to bolster you through to the end of your road trip. The same thing happens when you work towards a goal. When you see that the finish line really isn't as far as you initially thought, you find that reserve, that newfound energy. In fact, you may find that, as a result, you reach your goal quicker than planned. In *Before Happiness,* Shawn Achor calls this energy the x-spot. This is the point where you can see the finish line and where you encounter a success accelerant, the newfound reserve to get you to your end goal.

You also want to celebrate achievements. If I feel I did a particularly good job of achieving some lofty goals in a month, I will do something to treat myself. Maybe it means buying a new sports jacket. It could be a weekend in the mountains with my family. By treating you and allowing yourself license to celebrate, you stay motivated. When I wear that new sports jacket it always makes me think of success. It makes me hungry to reach more of my goals.

Make sure you read and review all of your goals on an ongoing basis. Review your one, three, and five-year goals at least monthly and more if possible. This will help you to continue to internalize the success you will attain. Make sure your goals are fluid. Perhaps four or five months into your year you realize that your one-year goals were not lofty enough. Perhaps another opportunity presents itself that will change your original goal set. That is fine. Take the time to go back and revise your one-year goals, or whatever goals are affected. You are the captain of this ship. You can do whatever you put your mind to doing.

It's Okay to Be a Capitalist Monk

I do a lot of talking about finding your destiny and about knowing your true self, being thankful and contributing to the world. It sounds very meditative and it truly is, but please don't think you have to be poor in order to do all of the above. You don't have to shave your head and go sit on a mountaintop to discover your true self and your destiny. On the contrary, it is absolutely fine to enjoy material things and to celebrate life by enjoying things that you can buy with your success if this is what you want to do. Having money certainly makes certain issues easier and it is not a sin to be wealthy. In fact, having money can free you up to pursue other positive endeavours, such as spending time with your family. Just always remember that you can't take it with you. Always have your priorities straight. Know what is most important. Money and success are great, but being remembered and leaving a legacy are much more important. You likely won't be remembered for all of the money you had, but you will be remembered for your deeds and it is a much longer lasting legacy to leave the world.

You may not immediately know your destiny. In fact, I would doubt that you do. As you heal yourself and take all responsibility for yourself, your destiny and opportunity will reveal itself to you. The world is an ever-changing place. None of us knows what tomorrow will bring. If you look back on your life I would bet that you would be surprised by some of the lows and highs that occurred. You didn't know they were coming. And so, too, your future is a mystery. Make your plans to become your best self. All of your future success rides on these plans. Make goals and work to achieve them, but do your best to keep your goals fluid and be ready to adapt. You may have heard the saying, "man plans and God laughs." This is life. Your goals may need to change and your destiny may be adjusted in another direction if need be. This is why you need to make time to think, plan and reflect on a regular basis. If you know your authentic self, you will be open to the many opportunities that will come your way.

This is what life brings us: change and opportunity. This is also how you learn your true destiny, through the journey itself. Remember to enjoy the journey. It never ends. Just as you get to the end of one road, another awaits your footsteps.

"If you don't know where you are going,
you'll end up someplace else."

- Yogi Berra

"While intent is the seed of manifestation, action is the water that nourishes the seed. Your actions must reflect your goals in order to achieve true success."

- Steve Maraboli, Life, the Truth, and Being Free

"While spirituality provides an efficient and endless fuel for your mind and body, you must burn that fuel with human action towards your goals, dreams, and desires."

- Steve Maraboli, Unapologetically You: Reflection on Life and the Human Experience

Chapter 9: Points for Self-Examination

- Don't just want; make true change.
- Find your "Why."
- Make a personal mission statement.
- What do you want to accomplish in your life?
- Goals are your compass to achievement.
- Write down your goals in detail.
- Write about the actual attainment of your goals.
- Break your goals down into five, three, one-year, and one-month goals with a weekly and daily task list focused on goal attainment.
- Focus your goals on the positive with positive statements.
- From time to time, look back at your progress.
- It's all right to be holistic and to be a capitalist.

Chapter 10

Reset

"If you believe you can change - if you make it a habit - the change becomes real."

- Charles Duhigg,

The Power of Habit: Why We Do What We Do in Life and Business

Routine Reason

The words routine and habit don't sound very exciting. Yet on some level this is how all of us live our lives on a daily basis. As I mentioned before, we are creatures of habit. How does one form a habit? First, you dedicate yourself to making a particular action a routine, doing it daily. Then it simply becomes a habit. It is what you do without fail. If you don't happen to complete the task when you are supposed to do it, you miss it. You wish you had done the task. Why? Because it has become a habit.

Lots of people bristle at the mention of a routine within their life. They feel they are free rather than having to contend with the same tasks day in and day out. Have you ever met a "lazy teenager?" Maybe they sleep in as late as possible. They want to stay in their pyjamas all day long. They play video games and eat junk food. Why would they want to get a job? They do these same things day in and day out. Whether they like it or not they have created a routine and have hence formed a habit (quite possibly a negative one at that). I'm not trying to give teenagers a rough ride here. I used to be this teenager at one point in time and this certainly does not describe all teenagers. This is merely for an example and I know there are driven teens all over the world that are loving life. I think you get the point though. All of us have routines or habits. Some are positive and some are negative. Show me a successful person and I will show you somebody with strict routine in his or her life. Everybody needs a system of execution and good routines turn into positive habits.

Think about the routines you have in your life. Are they beneficial to your successes or are they holding you back? Think about some routines you can add on a daily basis that will help you to succeed in the long run. Pick out some daily strategies to better help yourself achieve the goals you have set for yourself. At the same time, subtract the routines that are taking away from your successes. You may not even realize you are doing these detrimental things on a conscious level. Really examine what you might be doing that is not a positive factor to you reaching your goals. I don't mean stop going to your kid's soccer games three times a week. That is absolutely important if family is part of your "why." Perhaps you spend way too much time surfing the Internet or mindlessly manoeuvring through Facebook. That's the kind of stuff you want to eliminate or at least seriously curtail. You will be amazed at the time you can free up for positive routines.

People often say to me, "You must have a lot of will power in order to be doing these routines that you do." I don't really think of it in those terms. I think of them as successful strategies that allow me to accomplish my goals. In *The Compound Effect,* Darren Hardy refers to this as *why* power. Why do you want to make change? What is your motivation? I do these routines not because of will power, but because I have a *why*, I am motivated. Having a why is far better than will power. By using shear act of will you might not keep up with your routines or you might skip some of them. I don't because I know the deeper reasons I perform these tasks and the rewards are just too great to want to dismiss.

Time Block Values First

A good way to fit in all of the tasks you need to complete in any given day, week or month is to time block them into your calendar. It will help you to stay organized and will ensure you are accomplishing lots in any given day. Start by examining your values. What is most important to you? For me I know I want to excel at my business goals, but when I examine my values, first and foremost, I really want to be a present and attentive father and husband. Because this is of utmost importance to me, I time block time with my children into my weekly calendar and I do the same for time with my wife.

If a client wants me to meet them during these particular times, I apologize and let them know I have another appointment booked at this time and recommend a choice of a few other times.

Holidays are very important to me. First of all, it is important, uninterrupted time away with my family. Secondly, I require a recharge from time to time so that I can better keep my focus to achieve my goals. I fiercely guard these vacation times within my calendar.

Another important item to me is exercise. As I mentioned earlier, I prefer exercising mid-morning, but with a two busy pre-school children at home and other business items to attend to during the day, it is difficult for me to be able to workout at this time. So I time block exercise into my calendar early in the morning before my children and wife are awake. Believe me, this is where I need to create routine in order to fabricate a habit because I don't like getting up extra early to pump iron. But I do it and if I don't do it, I miss it. It is now my habit.

The other thing I like to do is to have time to read or listen to something motivational for at least fifteen minutes every day. I do this while I ride the bike during my workout time and if I don't ride the bike, then I read for fifteen minutes before bed. This was initially a part of my routine, but now it is habit. If I don't feed my mind and my psyche with this positive information on a daily basis, I really miss it. Doing it helps me to feel ready to conquer the world.

Some other important routines I started that are now habits are to make sure that I express my gratitude to my clients for their business. I always let them know how much I appreciate them and how I don't take our relationship for granted. I used to do this as a part of good business, but because I make a focus of expressing gratitude, I truly mean it. The good business part is merely a side effect of the practice itself.

Time Block Life After Values

Now that you have time blocked the items that are of utmost importance to you because they represent your values and priorities, you can now go about planning your days and weeks without any worry that you are cheating yourself of what you truly need and want. For example, based on my above values, I can schedule meetings, appointments, phone calls and tasks, and social outings wherever I can fit them in, and I do so with a clear and happy conscience because I have not interfered with my core values. By doing this, I know that I am being true to myself. It helps to ensure that I am a happy and well-balanced individual ready to fire on all cylinders.

Now because you have lists of goals, you can ensure that all of these tasks get done on a regular basis. Making these lists of goals, as I discussed earlier, is a routine that will eventually become habit. For me, I feel lost without these roadmaps that I create towards my greater success. These items are attended to in my calendar each day, but they do not in any way conflict with the times that I require for my greater values.

Motivation

I know all of this sounds very busy, but it is a good thing. By practicing these routines and making them habits, you end up getting a lot accomplished in a day. There is some truth to the old adage: if you want something to get done, ask a busy person. Being organized means being accomplished. By completing these small tasks on a daily basis, even though they may seem insignificant on a grander scale, you are able to accomplish huge goals that you set for yourself. Small, consistent contributions to a greater goal result in enormous results over a period of time. Try it and then look back over the past year and see all of the things you accomplished. I sometimes find myself knocking off a yearly goal in a month's time instead of a year because of the consistent steps I take on a daily basis. The power of small contributions on a regular basis can be absolutely staggering.

Think about it this way. If you are considering walking across the country, it can be daunting to think of the journey as a whole. Some people might not even begin the journey. The person that takes one hundred steps is one hundred steps further into the journey than the person that never started. If you plan to walk for a few hours every day and look back in a month's time, the distance you travelled will amaze you. A couple hours a day may not be overly taxing, but by doing it consistently every day, you conquer a good part of that journey.

Another way to help you stay on course with your routines is to let key people know what you are doing. Choose people that will hold your feet to the fire, so to speak. These people will help you to stay accountable in a positive manner. If you like, call these people your accountability partners. Perhaps you can do the same for them. You're not doing these routines for these individuals, but because they will be asking about your progress, it's best to be able to give them a positive report.

I'm not going to lie to you. It certainly helps to know your why for doing things, but success is not immediate. You need to be patient and if you are not staying motivated, then you may falter with some of your routines. Again, that's okay. All of us drop the ball from time to time. Don't beat yourself up. Practice self kindness and just get back to doing your routine and stick with it. Again, in *The Compound Effect,* Darren Hardy talks about momentum and its impact on incorporating routine and habit into your life for bringing continued success into it. Just like Newton's First Law, the Law of Inertia, so it is with routines. It may be tough to get started, but once you get going you will achieve some terrific results. All of us have likely looked at a successful person and marvelled at how they continue to be more and more successful, or the wealthy that become more and more wealthy. These people have put in place some positive routines for their successes and because of momentum and stick-ability to their routines, making them habits, momentum has continued to carry them through to greater and greater results. That's pretty exciting stuff!

Luck and Luxuries

Don't confuse success for luck. Every successful person, on whatever realm they are looking for success, have done so by having organized systems in place, such as goals and habits. Their successes may appear lucky to some, but it really has to do with being in the right state of mind and using proper systems. Remember, there is no such thing as an overnight sensation! Here is how luck is really discovered. You heal yourself and utilize gratitude to put yourself in the right state of mind. You prepare yourself using goals, routines, and habits in order to work towards what is important to you in your life. This is considered to be discipline. An opportunity comes along that you might otherwise not be able to realize had you not already done all of this previous preparation. Because you are now at peace and open to the world, and because you are disciplined in the field of what you want to accomplish, you are ready to seize that opportunity in the window that it presents itself. That's the true definition of luck. It is hard work, but it doesn't seem like it to an outsider. That's because really "lucky" people enjoy what they do and relish making their lives better and better. Another way of thinking of it is that these "lucky" people utilize the law of attraction – they see, experience, and get what they are looking for. Again, none of this is possible without the preparation already mentioned.

I've had some people say to me: "Patrick, you seem very holistic in what you are saying about getting yourself right and being open to the world, God, and the universe. And yet it seems conflicting to be putting in place routines and habits to bring about success in terms of monetary value." I've said it earlier and I will say it again: you can bring about success in your life in terms of monetary value or in other ways. What it truly comes down to is the importance to you as the individual. You can put your goals and thoughts out to the universe, but then you have to do the work, the actions, to bring them to you. I am a huge fan of Robin Sharma. I highly recommend you read his book, *Discover Your Destiny*. His viewpoint is similar to my own on this subject, which I touched upon earlier in this book. Whether you believe in God or the universe, man has been given intelligence to invent and create. These include material things. There is nothing wrong with striving to create and enjoy material things. Not all of us are meant to sit atop a mountaintop to meditate and take a vow of silence. Again, just remember your true values and priorities. I truly believe that if you choose, you can have everything in life. You can be an enlightened human being and wealthy at the same time.

Examine where you are today. Are you taking the steps toward your own personal happiness and inevitable successes? If yes, great! If not, hit the reset button today and watch how you start to flourish over a few short months.

"The secret of your success is found in your daily routine."

- John C. MaxWell

"Motivation is what gets you started. Habit is what keeps you going."

- Jim Ryun

Chapter 10: Points for Self-Evaluation

- **Create positive habits through the use of routine.**
- **Don't focus on the use of will power when starting a routine, rather focus on your "why;" your values.**
- **Time block your values first; what is most important to you!**
- **Time block your life after your values.**
- **Use strategies to stay motivated.**
- **Don't confuse success for luck.**

Chapter 11

Fly

"Change will not come if we wait for some other person, or if we wait for some other time. We are the ones we've been waiting for. We are the change that we seek."

- Barack Obama

Step Out of Your Comfort Zone

As human beings we tend to be creatures of habit. All of us have patterns that we adhere to on a daily basis in some way, shape, or form. For many of us these patterns are about comfort. For others, these patterns can be about complacency. If you are doing the same things day in and day out, you will bring about the same results.

Have you always dreamed about living in Belize? Perhaps you want to start your own company. Maybe you want to spend more time with your family. Why can't you? Don't limit your potential. You can do anything. You simply need to start moving forward. Let go of your self-limiting beliefs. Find your true self and realize the power that you hold within your very being.

Many people won't try new things because of a fear that it won't work out. They are afraid that if they step out of their box and try something different, they won't like it or it won't work out, or at the very least it won't be as good as what they are currently doing. Even if they don't like what they are currently doing and long for better results they won't change. These are the same people that often complain about their current situation, but won't take the steps to make it better. These same individuals are the ones that may tell you that your dreams are unattainable. Think about the alternative here: you just continue on, getting by, and continue to be unhappy. My friend, I again refer you back to what Mr. Einstein said about insanity. I'm telling you that you cannot have what you long for if you aren't willing to try something different.

You've likely heard that it is better to have loved and lost than to never have loved at all. What about truly living the life you were supposed to live? At the end of your life, how will you reflect on how you lived? Did you give it your all and live to the fullest, attaining your true destiny, or did you stick to the comfortable even though it really never made you happy or gave you a zest for your life? At the end I really want you to say that your life was an incredible journey and that you know you lived your destiny and made the world a better place. This is the long-term gain you will have for conquering the short-term pain which is your fear of doing something different and living your destiny.

I challenge you to differentiate yourself. Make what you do on a daily basis different than that of what the vast majority of the world does on a daily basis. To be truly happy and successful, you need to do what others are not willing to do. You need to take action. Step out of your comfort zone and do it often. A journey starts with a few small steps, and then another, and then another. While seemingly daunting at first, consistency will lead you to huge results in a shorter amount of time than you ever dreamed possible. Soon your steps will lead you to greater and greater results and then you will no longer be walking. You will be flying.

Don't Give Up

If you decide that you aren't happy doing what you are currently doing and you decide to make change, then first accept that life will not be the same. There will be some discomfort at first. This is because you will be doing something out of the norm of what you are used to doing and this will move you outside of your comfort zone. And know that there will be naysayers and people who will not support you on this. Remember that this journey is about you, not them.

As an example of an individual moving through this discomfort, consider someone that is just starting a resistance or weight-training program. At the beginning, it is a big change. The individual experiences pain in their muscles because it is something they have either never done or have not done in a while. It's easy to give up in the beginning because of this initial pain and the shake up to the system, but if they stick with it, the pain goes away after a few days.

After a few months the person may not see a whole lot of results. Again, it might be easy to give up, but if they stick with it a little longer, say 4 or 6 months, they will start to see huge improvements in their health and in their physique. Small efforts practiced daily can lead to big results. It takes discipline.

True change takes effort. There is no magic pill. It is not easy. Anything worth doing rarely is. Have trust in the values that are the center point of your goals. Things may not be as good as they currently are for you, but they could become even greater for you if you focus, and they will. If you really want change, then you will endure and you will reap all of the rewards for doing so.

Make Broad Changes

Nobody is perfect. I urge you to make the earlier discussed goals for your life multi-faceted. Make broad changes. Don't go for easy. Work on your personal goals, family goals, health goals, career goals, etc. There is a good reason for this kind of approach. Not only will it help you to grow and improve in many areas of your life, but you will also find that some goals in certain areas will be more quickly attainable. By doing this, you will be less deterred if some of your goals don't come to fruition as quickly as you originally hoped. That's all right. We live and learn by trial and error. By seeing improvements in some areas of your life, you will be more likely to continue to be consistent with working towards progress in the areas that may be lagging. You will be buoyed by the success you do see. You will see that consistency does bring results and that you may need to be a little more patient with some of your objectives.

What happens if you make change and it doesn't work out, such as trying a different career path or changing your workplace? You keep trying. Try something different with your career path. You just did it once so try it again. Maybe tweak what you are doing. If you moved places of employment, you can move again. What matters at the end of the day is your accountability to yourself. Give yourself kudos for trying and try again. Remember that failure is really just experience. So, move onto the next experience. Remember that you are now in pursuit of your true destiny and it is a journey. You wouldn't drive five kilometres of a planned six hundred kilometre journey and then give up because you had to stop to go to the bathroom. Good for you for taking the first steps. Now take a few more steps.

Now what happens if you make change and it does work out? You will start to see progress towards your goals. You will absolutely see results if you practice what I have laid out for you here in this book. That's exciting! Remember that life happens and things may not always work out as you plan, but that is why you must be willing to be flexible and adapt to the change. Keep your eyes open to opportunity. When you pursue what you truly want, doors will open that you didn't know would open. You may find opportunities that are adjunctive to what you want to accomplish, or may find them more appealing and do them instead. That's okay too. That's the beauty of the journey; it's not boring. It's not doing the same thing day in and day out, knowing that it really isn't what you want. It's doing things over and over again because you want to do them. You want the results that badly. It's the pursuit of your values and happiness. Even after you reach your goal, there will be a new opportunity waiting for you and you can pick and choose those opportunities and make them work for you.

Believe

I know I'm speaking in generalities. The truth is that whatever you want in life, make the change and get ready to get dirty. Knowing this will happen is enough to get you through. Try enough and you will absolutely succeed. The act of making the change is part of the true enjoyment of change. It's an adventure! Maybe the grass really is greener on the other side. The truth is that you will never know until you get there. There are no guarantees, but if you continue to play small and don't have the courage to make a plan and try, then that is on you. All of us are responsible for our own lives. We are exactly where we are right now in our lives because of the choices we made. Perception or not, we are accountable for our own happiness. If you long for betterment, then don't be afraid to open yourself up to trying something different. All of us have so much untapped potential. Know that there is so much more to you than what you see in the mirror today.

Believe! You are a unique and intelligent individual with unlimited potential. You can do anything you put your mind to doing if you do all of the work to simply make it happen. Believe in you! I'm your biggest supporter. I know you can succeed. Be happy and enjoy all of the success you truly deserve. Savour the journey ahead and remember to have fun! The power lies within you. You alone are responsible. Wake up, transform, and flourish throughout your life. It's time for you to attain the wealth you deserve and live large!

"We are taught you must blame your father, your sisters, your brothers, the school, the teachers - but never blame yourself. It's never your fault. But it's always your fault, because if you wanted to change you're the one who has got to change."

- Katherine Hepburn, Me: Stories of My Life

"We can't be afraid of change. You may feel very secure in the pond that you are in, but if you never venture out of it, you will never know that there is such a thing as an ocean, a sea. Holding onto something that is good for you now, may be the very reason why you don't have something better."

- C. JoyBell C.

"Destiny is not a matter of chance; it is a matter of choice. It is not a thing to be waited for, it is a thing to be achieved."

- Williams Jennings Bryan

Chapter 11: Points for Self-Evaluation

- **Embrace Change.**
- **At the end of your life, how will you reflect upon how you lived it?**
- **Small efforts practiced daily lead to huge results.**
- **Keep your values as the center point for your goals.**
- **Make your goals, your changes, multi-faceted.**
- **Believe and enjoy the journey.**

WTF:

A Brief Re-Cap

Now that you have read up to this point, you will have a very good idea of the steps you need to take to attain the life you deserve and live large. I will further break down the entire book from Wake up to Transform to Flourish to assist you with the major talking points.

W: Wake Up

First, you need to overcome your story. Each one of us lives our own story. We've been places. We've had things happen to us. We have our own perceptions. Sometimes, one feels beat up and battered by life in general. Remember that this is a perception. Perhaps you are that square peg trying to fit into a round hole. Perhaps you are really living somebody else's story as opposed to creating and living your own story. You need to find a way to be brave enough to make changes for you.

Let go of past experiences and false perceptions. What is your past is past. Don't let it beat you up any longer. If there is a negative experience from your past, perceived or not, that is haunting you, take the lesson that can be found in the experience and extract all that you can learn from it and then put it behind you for good. You are not your past. Don't let it affect you. You are not a victim.

Be an active participant in your life. Don't let somebody else write your story. Be ready to seize control. To do so, you must first identify what are your true values and priorities in life. Once you have a clear picture of what is of most importance to you, then you can wake up and align the rest of your life with those values.

Be prepared to fail and fail often. This is from Chapter 2 **Burn and Learn**. It's all right to have a few failures under your belt. In fact, they are terrific learning experiences. Allow yourself licence to fail and don't beat yourself up over them. In fact, don't call them failures. Simply call them experiences.

Seek the positive in all things. Remember that thoughts lead to actions. So concentrate on positive thoughts and your actions will follow suit. Try to add positives to your mind and body. This means associating with like-minded people, reading positive material and listening to positive material.

Eliminate worry and fear from your consciousness and make sure it does not creep into your subconscious. These are useless and detrimental emotions that are given way too much attention. They are harmful to you as a person, including your productivity and your health. Listen to your body. It can tell you when you are worried or fearful. You can't predict the future and if you could, why would you include worry and fear? Punt it from your life! Learn to manage worry and fear.

Perceptions of relationships past and present can hold you back. Examine if you are overly influenced by a relationship. Is it positive or negative? Is your perception of the relationship a true representation or are you viewing it incorrectly? Having the skill of deciphering good from bad will better help you to move forward in your personal growth and lead your own story.

Recognize if you were raised in an autocratic or democratic household. The leadership style within the home in which you were raised can have an effect on who you are and how you interact with others. This does not mean that this is who you have to be, but knowing can assist you to make changes within yourself and better your interpersonal relationships should it be required.

Build your confidence. As you build your level of confidence, you are better able to embrace the idea that you can make great changes within your own life. This means you are the star of your own story.

Always look for relationships that are empowering to you as a person. You want supportive and symbiotic relationships. These are people that support you and embrace the change you want to make. At the same time recognize chronic situations that sabotage your growth. Don't put yourself in these same situations day in and day out. Stop all together. They are not beneficial to you as a person.

T: Transform

Realize that you are the most important person to you! You need to look after yourself first and foremost before you can be of true help to anybody else. For this reason, you need to be kind to yourself. Be kind in your internal dialogue as you go about your day. It's like speaking to your grandmother. You wouldn't sass her (hopefully)! Speak kindly to you.

Stay focused on the positive. If you want to eliminate personal debt, don't focus on the personal debt. You don't want more of it. Instead focus on making money and debt will take care of itself. Do similarly to other areas of your life. Don't think about not gaining weight. Think about being healthy.

Look after you as the total package. Yes, focus on enriching your mind, but also look after your diet and your health. Eliminate negative influences and instead replace them with positive influences.

Invest in you. This could mean buying exercise equipment to buying excellent self-development books. Maybe you want to enlist the expertise of a coach to help you to reach your personal goals. This could be a personal trainer to a business coach to a life coach. The point is that the investment in you is money well spent. Remember that what you think results in actions, so think and grow to a better you.

Success does not create happiness. Happiness creates success. Part of being happy means that you can shift your daily viewpoint, your perception of other people. So many individuals go about their day in anger. Don't be affected by them. Recognize the hurt they feel and the power they try to inflict upon you disappears.

Don't take the easy societal viewpoint of people and situations. It takes effort to rise above those societal perceptions. This will also be good practice for you to perceive a reality where others do not, and will, in turn, allow you to achieve.

Take time to be thankful. Be thankful for what you have in your life and the supportive people around you. Be thankful for the goals you are going to achieve, even though they may not yet have come to fruition. Doing this betters your state of mind and makes you more open to the positives around you. It will accelerate your own personal growth and goal attainment. Never underestimate the power and impact of the words, "thank you. These are relationship-building words. Being thankful brings so much good into your life if practiced with regularity. Find time each and every day to practice gratitude.

There are no coincidences. Things happen for a reason, and often we don't have the capacity to understand how we play a role in these so-called "coincidences." We, as humans, are incredible beings with so much potential. The majority of people don't come close to accessing even small levels of this potential. The power of the subconscious mind is absolutely staggering. If you have unwavering belief, and internalize this belief in your subconscious mind, then you can bring about the outcome of your belief. Vibrate your convictions of your goal attainment to the universe. Believe as though it is already done. Your thoughts, when combined with proper actions, will bring about the result. You have the power within you to do anything, to achieve anything, by utilizing the power of your subconscious mind.

F: Flourish

You can't simply want change. You must make change. Find your "why," your deeper meaning. What are your values? What is most important to you? Write a mission statement so you never lose focus of your values. Find out what you want to accomplish in your life.

Now create your goals. They become your compass to achievement. It is not enough simply to have goals rolling around in your head. If they are not written down in detail, then they are merely hopes and wishes. Write down your goals into five, three, one-year and one-month increments. Also keep a weekly and daily task list that directly relates to the attainment of your goals. Don't forget to write passionately about your five, three, and one-year goals. Include how their attainment makes you feel and what you will be doing. Internalize their completion. Make sure your goals are written in the positive with positive statements. Review them on a regular basis. Don't forget to look back at your progress and see where you have come from in your journey towards your goal attainment. You will be astounded at your progress. Don't forget, it is all right to be holistic and a capitalist. You can do and be both!

Create positive habits in your daily life through the use of routine. Don't focus on will power to create these habits, but focus on your "why," your values. Time block your day effectively for more efficient attainment of your goals. Time block your values first. This means that you first make time daily for things that are of most importance to you. Next, time block life. Use strategies to keep you motivated every day.

Don't confuse success for luck. It's easy to look at those with great success as being "lucky" and then to become discouraged, thinking you can't do the same things. Luck is the result of preparation and planning meeting opportunity. These individuals are skilled at doing the things I am teaching you in this book. You too can be successful and appear "lucky" to others.

Finally, embrace change. At the end of your life, how will you reflect on how you lived it? It is my wish for you that you will be able to say that you lived it well. I hope you can say your life was full. Don't play small. Make your life count.

Keep your values as the center point for your goals. Make your goals multi-faceted, working to achieve on many levels. Remember that small efforts practiced daily lead to huge results. Have unwavering belief in the attainment of your goals and enjoy the adventure!

WTF!

Wake Up, Transform, and Flourish!

Closing

I hope you have enjoyed reading this book as much as I have enjoyed putting it together. If you can say that you walked away with even one tidbit of information that excited you and reso`nated with you, then I consider my quest to impart this knowledge I have learned, to be a success.

As human beings we are always learning. Never stop learning. Never stop reading and trying to find more knowledge to better yourself and those around you. To use the gifts you have learned, and to be of service to others, is the noblest act in the world and it is also the most rewarding. Take the knowledge you learn to make things better for others, whatever that may look like in your situation.

Know that I am your biggest supporter. I know that, because you are reading this book, you want to achieve more. If you enjoyed this book, please pass it on! If you want to accelerate your growth further, know that I am here to help! Keep growing and watch your life explode into greatness. You can have it all! You are worth it!

Need a keynote speaker for an event? Do you want one on one distance coaching? Contact Patrick Murray.

Some Gratitude

Accomplishment always comes with assistance and having the support of others is a gift that I don't take lightly. If you are open and ready, teachers appear when you need them. I am the proof that this is truth.

Thank you to my wonderful wife, Colette. You are my rock and you are the strongest person I know. Never once did you complain when I was unable to assist with our children because I just couldn't stop writing. You are my soul mate. You too are an entrepreneur and you achieve every day. Thank you for your example and thank you for being number one in my top five, even if we are married! Okay... My top two. I'm an introvert.

Thank you to my son, Declan. You are a teacher that teaches me every day at the ripe age of four! You are my shift. You make me realize how much more I can be just by being you. I admire your energy and I look at you and remember that yes, it is important to goal set and strive for future accomplishment, but that it is so important to savour now! I want to be the kind of man that you will say you want to be! Thank you for making me better.

To my baby girl, Lyric, that is, as of the time of writing, 8 months old; thank you for coming into our lives. You are our miracle baby and whenever I look at you I can't help but smile. Thank you for that. I look forward to all that you will teach me. Be gentle with Daddy!

Thank you to my friends and family that knew I was writing a book. I know I chose the right people to associate with because never once did any of you tell me I couldn't do it. I never felt an ounce of doubt from any of you and you don't know what that support means to me. Thank you!

Thank you to Shawn Shewchuk, Change Your Results. I truly value being able to bounce my many ideas off of you. You are a husband, a father, a businessman, an author, and the list goes on. Thank you for understanding the importance of family and work/life balance. Thank you for challenging me to write this book. I am thankful that I can call you my friend.

To my editor, Lindsay Harle from The Write Harle, thank you for your patience with the edits on my end and for deciphering the ramblings of an inspired man. You are a lovely human being and are so good at what you do.

Finally, thank you to you! Thank you for taking some lessons from a formerly bruised and battered soul that learned I could achieve anything and have everything. Thank you for the gift of allowing me to impart a little bit of knowledge to make you and your life better. I look forward to being an ongoing resource for you and others!

Appendix

Achor, Shawn. *Before Happiness*. New York, New York: Crown Business, 2013.

Byrne, Rhonda. *The Secret*. Hillsboro, Oregon: Beyond Words Publishing, 2006.

Covey, Steven R. *The 7 Habits of Highly Effective People*. New York, New York: Free Press Publishing, 2004.

Hardy, Darren. *The Compound Effect*. New York, New York: Vanguard Press, 2010.

Hill, Napolean. *Think and Grow Rich*. New York, New York: Penguin Group, 2005.

Sharma, Robin. *Discover Your Destiny With The MonkWho Sold His Ferrari*. Toronto, Ontario: Harper Collins Publishers Ltd, 2008.

Tolle, Eckart. *The Power of Now - A Guide to Spiritual Enlightenment*. Vancouver, British Columbia: Namaste Publishing, 2004.

Tracy, Brian. *The Psychology of Achievement Classic*. Niles, Illinois: Nightingale Conant.

www.ingramcontent.com/pod-product-compliance
Lightning Source LLC
LaVergne TN
LVHW051837080426
835512LV00018B/2934